Education and the Market Place

Education and the Market Place

Edited by

David Bridges and Terence H. McLaughlin

 The Falmer Press

(A member of the Taylor & Francis Group)
London • Washington, D.C.

UK	The Falmer Press, 4 John Street, London WC1N 2ET
USA	The Falmer Press, Taylor & Francis Inc., 1900 Frost Road, Suite 101, Bristol, PA 19007

First published in 1994

A catalogue record for this book is available from the British Library

Library of Congress Cataloging-in-Publication Data are available on request

ISBN 0 7507 0348 2 cased
ISBN 0 7507 0349 0 paper

Jacket design by Caroline Archer

Typeset in 10/12pt Bembo by
Graphicraft Typesetters Ltd., Hong Kong.

Printed in Great Britain by Burgess Science Press, Basingstoke on paper which has a specified pH value on final paper manufacture of not less than 7.5 and is therefore 'acid free'.

Contents

Content

Chapter 1

Education and the Market Place: An Introduction

David Bridges and Terence H. McLaughlin

In the United Kingdom the administrations of Conservative Prime Ministers Margaret Thatcher and John Major have shared a conviction that almost any function of society — from the economy to health care, from telephones to the custody of criminals — may be enhanced if these functions are performed under conditions as close as possible to those of the market place. As several of the chapters in this book will illustrate, these same policies have been viewed with favour in many parts of the world.

The main conditions required to satisfy this ideal have included:

- the breaking up or weakening of state or other monopolies so as to provide a choice of service provider for customers and competition between providers;
- the removal of state support and subsidies from providers, so that there is a 'purer' form of competition allowing whichever provider is genuinely the most efficient to succeed;
- the provision of reliable information to consumers (e.g., in the form of accurate and comprehensive descriptions of goods or comparative data about the costs and performance of competing service providers); and
- the creation of real opportunities for choice and an appreciation of that opportunity for choice among consumers.

Of course a commitment to the creation of these conditions has also required other social and political changes in the United Kingdom. It is doubtful that these changes could have been introduced in the public service sector for example if the government had not first significantly weakened the power of the trade unions. The selling off of the state monopoly of the mining industry to the private sector could not have proceeded before the power of the National Union of Mineworkers had been attacked, and indeed the issue of privatization was central to their struggle with the government. Nor were, for example, the health workers' unions or the teachers' unions in any real position by the end of the 1980s to mount concerted or sustained opposition to government policies.

The changes also required a significant shift in the population's ideological thinking about, for example, the locus of responsibility in society for the care of the sick or the elderly, the provision of transport to rural areas or of training and continuing education. What had hitherto been regarded as the rather noble and civilized institution of the Welfare State was systematically disparaged in many political quarters as the 'nanny' state supporting a 'dependency culture'. In its place were offered the new entrepreneurialism, the 'enterprise culture', the promise that wealth created at one level of society would eventually filter down to the benefit of all and, in rather uneasy partnership with this public celebration of self-interest, a reaffirmation of the family as the central locus of social care and responsibility.

It was Kenneth Clarke who was entrusted to carry these policies into three major departments of state: Health and Social Security, Education and then the Home Office, and he did so with zealous enthusiasm. Many of us in education and elsewhere had become persuaded in the 1970s of the importance in the educational change process of, for example, a careful basis of consultation; of enabling those who would have responsibility for carrying change through to contribute creatively to the shaping of that change and to feel some ownership of it; of the need to support people in the change process with training and consultancy; of the importance of formative evaluation in monitoring the effects of change and modifying the development in the light of this information. If Kenneth Clarke had heard of this collective wisdom on educational innovation he clearly chose like his predecessor as Secretary of State for Education, Kenneth Baker, to ignore it. Had he thought at all in these terms he would no doubt have concluded that even if such approaches might engage the support of those who had to operate a changed system, it would be at the price of some considerable subversion of the original agenda. Instead, his approach to educational reform was consistently based upon (i) the accruing of regulatory power to his own office (the main function of successive Education Acts); (ii) the undermining of any groupings that might present serious political opposition (the unions, the local education authorities); (iii) the division of the service sector he was addressing into units standing in competitive relations with each other; and (iv) the offering of financial incentives to those who led the way in taking on the new ideology and operating conditions (e.g., grant maintained schools or in the case of the Health Service trust hospitals). In a context of high unemployment and low job security many employees at all levels were understandably ready to put any allegiance to the former order second to their need to establish themselves in the new one.

The main manifestations of the application of this policy to the education system reflect closely the four conditions with which we started. They include:

- the breaking up of 'the LEA monopoly' of schooling through the introduction of grant maintained schools and continued support for independent schools through an assisted-places scheme;
- the publication of more and comparative information about school performance with a view to informing consumer choice, with parents seen as the consumers;
- the provision for greater flexibility in school admissions so as to allow greater opportunity for parents to send their children to the school of their choosing;
- provision for members of the business community to bring their approaches and skills to the management of schools as school governors;
- the opening up of a whole range of services traditionally provided by LEAs to competition from private agencies, including privatized agencies from other LEAs — these have included everything from school cleaning, catering and gardening, through advisory and support services to personnel, payroll and architectural services;
- the opening up of school inspection to a variety of agencies competing for work on the basis of competitive tendering; and
- the introduction of elements of competitive tendering into higher education (which was already operating to some extent in a market as far as student choice of course and institution was concerned).

Simultaneously there has been a welter of government and independently inspired initiatives directed at the school and further and higher education curriculum and intended to prepare the next generation to operate with familiarity and commitment in the new market environment: the Technical and Vocational Education Initiative in schools, mini-enterprise projects, school–business partnerships and in higher education the Enterprise in Higher Education Initiative.

With all these developments has come the new educational vocabulary of 'customers' and 'service delivery'; of 'marketing' and 'promotion'; of 'the chief executive' and the 'business plan'; of 'cost control' and 'quality assurance'. What are we to make of all this — we parents, we governors, we teachers and headteachers, we citizens and taxpayers, we pupils and students, the citizens of tomorrow? Has the education system at last been brought to sanity and the real world? Will it be reinvigorated and made more effective by the application of market principles? Or is all this an ideologically-led perversion of a system which needs to be governed by quite different economic and social principles?

This book provides a variety of responses to these questions from people who, for the most part, work inside the education system and have experienced these changes at first hand. Their responses are a mixture of enthusiasm and scepticism, hope and disenchantment, pragmatism and principled protest tempered by a sustaining professional commitment to do the best possible job as they conceive it for the pupils of today and tomorrow in whatever political environment is provided.

We begin this volume with a look back in time, to the provision of public education in the period 1833–1944. This is not just a ritualistic nod in the direction of history. A lot of the arguments about the necessity or otherwise of state provision of education hark back to the nineteenth century and the gradual extension of the role of the State in educational provision alongside and perhaps at the expense of provision by the churches, by independent foundations and by private subscription. Philip Gardner describes the movement away from the nineteenth-century principle of separate, self-contained and unrelated subsystems of schooling towards the principle of a single, national, educational system, from a system dominated by market supply to a system dominated by central provision and regulation. He observes with particular poignancy the transfer of working-class allegiance from a growing system of private schools supported by the wages of the working classes to a state system in which the fulfilment of individual opportunity for all seemed possible.

Part 1 of the collection addresses different applications of market principles in practice. Geoff Morris and Donald Naismith both write as recently retired directors of local education authority services which have spearheaded many of the recent structural changes. While he was chief education officer in Cambridgeshire Geoff Morris pioneered the delegation of financial and other managerial responsibilities to schools, placing many of his own authority's services in a new relationship with schools, which could now choose what services they wished to buy from whom. Rosalie Clayton acknowledges in her chapter that Cambridgeshire schools were thus especially well equipped to take on the further responsibilities which fell to them with grant maintained status. Morris describes the impact of recent legislation on LEAs and the ways in which they have adapted to new market conditions. Central in the adaptations is the establishment out of old LEA services of new 'agencies' selling their services not only to schools but also (for example in the case of finance, personnel and information technology) to the authority itself or to others among its departments. Morris acknowledges the positive benefits which have come out of the new relationships with schools: the increased awareness of the need for efficiency, financial management of a high order and a 'close-to-customer' approach to the people the authorities exist to serve. At the same time, however, he observes two areas of the traditional LEA function which are inadequately served by the new educational market. The first of these is support for the individual who is getting poorly or unfairly treated by the system; the second is strategic planning. There remains, though government does not seem yet to recognize this, an important function for local government in both these areas.

Under Donald Naismith, Wandsworth LEA earned a reputation as an enthusiastic supporter of the government's educational initiatives and often paved the way in its own practices for what was subsequently to become government policy. He remains an advocate of the educational voucher as the means to give all parents equal access to a genuine choice of school inside or outside the state sector and he writes in particular on the basis of a recent study visit to see such a scheme in operation in Russia.

Rosalie Clayton and Peter Downes write as headteachers managing schools in the new market environment. Rosalie Clayton led her school buoyantly into its current grant maintained status convinced of the potential and challenges which 'self-determination' would offer. Describing her experience she slips easily into market analogies:

> The process of becoming grant maintained has similarities with the risks of floating a company on the stock market. The initial flotation depends, to a large degree on its reputation and ability to create shareholder confidence in the company and its future. The survival of the company after that is dependent on keeping its shareholders and customers happy.

Clayton describes the process of becoming grant maintained, the issues this raised and her experience of making grant maintained status work. Among the benefits she claims are tighter control over overheads (and hence a capacity to focus expenditure on teaching and learning) and a closer relationship between the school and parents. She shares some of Morris's concerns about the wider planning role of the LEA but believes that such problems can be solved in a spirit of cooperation between local self-managing schools. The role of the LEA is therefore, in her view, redundant.

Peter Downes acknowledges the discomfort of what he believes to be the majority of headteachers with the application of the concept of the market place to the school sector. However he also puts forward a more positive and perhaps acceptable interpretation of what it might mean in practice. He suggests for example that marketing does not mean trying to sell a product but being increasingly sensitive to the needs of the customers; recognizing that the days when schools had predetermined packages and immutable practices to offer pupils have gone. Schools must present themselves properly to parents and to the local community. He explores the implications of these and other expectations for the role of the headteacher and then finally poses the dilemma the head is in in recognizing a responsibility both to his or her own school and (with reference, again, to strategic planning and to 'the wider good') to the broader system of which the school is a part.

David Bridges focuses on the relationship between parents and school inside and outside the market model and reviews some of the competing conceptualizations of that relationship — of parents as: bystanders, supporters, partners, governors, coeducators and customers. He examines both the issues of principle underlying these different views and the evidence of the impact of the development of different relationships on children's learning. He argues that attempts to put parents in the role of customer for an educational service provided by the school is a retrogressive step in the light of the evidence from, and arguments for, a relationship based on a collaborative partnership in the education of a child.

The last two chapters in Part 1 consider some different issues. These are to do with the relations between the business community and schools. Peter Roberts writes as a head who for over fifteen years has developed close and supportive relations between his school and the local business community. He acknowledges the need of schools for funding and resources additional to that which comes from the local authority or government and hence the vulnerability of schools to commercial exploitation. He describes some of the different kinds of relationships which his own and other schools have established with local and national companies and the benefits which can be derived from them by both parties. He considers the question 'By what criteria should we assess whether business influence upon schools is exploitative rather than beneficent and supportive?' and argues in particular for local sustained partnerships in which schools take a proactive stance and affirm their own values with confidence.

Sheila Harty (a former 'Nader raider' for those readers who remember the David versus Goliath battles between this famous consumer leader and major American corporations) looks at this whole matter from a transatlantic perspective and with a plainly articulated scepticism. She highlights the intense interest among sales and marketing divisions of major corporations and of 'hucksters' acting on their behalf in the captive audience of pupils in schools, the extraordinary steps which corporations are taking to reach that market and the risks to pupils and to professional educational principles that these incursions represent. She offers some practical principles intended to govern schools' response to this predatory behaviour.

It will be clear from the discussion of the issues which is to be found in Part 1 of this book that the professional and public debate about the application of market principles to educational provision raises serious and complex issues of social, economic and political principle. There are issues concerning individual freedom and choice, social equity, notions of the public good, the location of responsibility for the care and education of children, the rights and duties of parents, of children and of the wider community; there are issues concerning the role and responsibilities of the State and the claims of the values of individualism and of community; and there are issues concerning the way in which we can or should resolve the many conflicting claims and imperatives of these different principles.

It is to these issues, which have a wide-ranging philosophical resonance, that we turn in Part 2 of the book. The contributors here are mainly writers in the field of philosophy of education, though Gerald Grace's roots are in the sociology and politics of education.

Colin Wringe returns to Adam Smith and 'The Wealth of Nations' for one of the two visions of the market place which he explores, but he argues that Smith and his followers failed to recognize circumstances in which the unrestricted operation of the free market or dependence on it is unlikely to prove beneficial: when activities are inherently detrimental to the public interest or subversive of essential social institutions; when market transactions are unsuitable for the distribution of necessities which individuals are unable to meet through no fault of their own or which are beyond the means of ordinary individuals; and when individuals are unqualified to judge their own needs or the quality of the services being offered. Starting from these principles, Wringe argues that education is inappropriately treated as a market commodity but should return to its status as a public service.

John White's attack on the application of market principles to education is built around a discussion of the influential writing of the American duo, Chubb and Moe, who seek a minimal role for the State in the determination of the curriculum, in the ownership of schools and in the allocation of children to schools. In all these areas, they argue, the market should rule. After a discussion of the claims of parents and children to be the relevant consumers in the context of curriculum decisions, White argues (in line with the Conservative government in this respect) that the rights of decision here lie not simply with those who happen to be pupils or parents but with citizens and hence the State. As far as ownership of schools is concerned, White's position is that the crucial consideration is not who owns the school but whether the school conforms to certain criteria of adequacy, and it is up to the State to enforce these. On choice of schooling, White expresses some sympathy for an element of parental choice, but on the grounds that parents are educators. This yields certain parental responsibilities rather than 'consumer rights'.

Gerald Grace's contribution to this volume also brings an international perspective to the discussion drawn from his own experience in New Zealand and his arguments against a policy document on education produced for the in-coming Labour government by economists of the New Zealand Treasury. The case which Grace develops here is that education is 'a public good' and that, this being so, it should be provided primarily by the State and without direct charge to all citizens. He concludes that:

> it does seem improbable that market culture which in its operation puts market before community; which necessarily maximizes strategies for individual profit and advantage; which conceptualizes the world in terms of consumers rather than citizens and which marginalizes issues to do with morality and ethics, will be the appropriate culture in which education as a public good can most effectively be provided.

After these assaults on market principles, it is left to James Tooley (in this case in a chapter written from, and with some particular reference to education in, South Africa) to articulate a philosophical defence of those principles — one which addresses in particular some of the arguments of Grace with whom he has already had a number of exchanges. Tooley sets up a model of a stable society functioning under the rule of law in which the State is only involved in education in the following ways: (i) it sets standards of what is deemed a 'minimum adequate education'; (ii) it licenses an inspectorate to ensure that educational establishments meet these standards; (iii) it authorizes established charities to ascertain those families who cannot afford to provide adequate educational opportunities for their children and provides bursaries to these families to be used in inspected establishments; (iv) it compels those children who are not partaking of the minimum adequate educational opportunities to do so. He then asks what might constitute principled objections to this position and addresses both the 'public good' argument articulated by Grace and arguments from the principle of equity put forward by, among others, Williams and Rawls. For Tooley it is not the creation of education markets which needs justification but the intervention of the State in education. As he points out, the debate about markets in education has been initiated in part because of dissatisfaction with state schooling. The question he wants to prompt is the wisdom of allowing states into areas of our lives where, as he sees it, they have no business.

Finally, in the concluding contribution to this section, Terence H. McLaughlin reviews some of the main issues raised in these chapters, in the broader literature generated by policy-development groups of different political persuasions and in the rich vein of literature on this topic in applied philosophy. Out of this he develops his own proposal that in a democracy certain higher-order values relevant to education and schooling ought to be exempt from market forces and regarded as a non-negotiable feature of all education and schooling.

The application of market principles to educational provision and practice represents a fundamental shift in our social as well as our educational culture. It is crucial that people inside and outside the educational system understand the full implications of this shift as these are worked out in schools and in local communities, that they understand both the practical consequences of the shift and the values which are promoted or lost in the process. Such understanding provides the basis for informed and considered resistance to, or implementation of, the changes. The authors will have made clear their own positions on these issues. We hope this book will help the reader to do the same.

Chapter 2

Schooling, Markets and Public Agency 1833–1944

Philip Gardner

At the beginning of the nineteenth century, there were still some for whom the idea of education for all was anathema. For such the prospect of an educated populace carried a threat rather than a promise (Sutherland, 1971, p. 9). In the maintenance of social order and national prosperity, popular ignorance was preferable to popular learning. This was a view for which support receded with every passing year of the new century. Within two or three decades it was quite extinct. Through the remainder of the century and into the next, the progressive 'rise of the schooled society' was assured (Wardle, 1974). In 1880 elementary schooling became compulsory and within a generation compulsion was simply an unquestioned assumption of social life. But as one capital question was resolved, another and far more intractable one took its place. This was a question which was not to be resolved so quickly — indeed it has remained a matter of periodically intense debate for the last 150 years. Though there have been occasions during this time when resolution has seemed close, the contemporary moment is not one of them. The question, debated with renewed vigour today, is that which asks by which agency or mechanism education should most appropriately be made available to its beneficiaries. It asks, in other words, about the place to be played by the market; and it asks about the place to be played by responsible public authority. The chapters in this book give their answers with an eye to the educational needs of today and tomorrow, but as they do so, it is worth remembering that they, in their turn, are also contributing to a much larger debate over time. The purpose of this chapter is to consider some aspects of the debate as it was negotiated by generations of our recent ancestors.

The Idea of National Education

There are many important turning points in this history, but there is one that stands above all others. It is not a turning point that we can associate with a single event or a single individual or group. It was a change which sprang from many sources, each reinforcing the other and coming together to develop a momentum affecting the whole life of the nation. Some of these sources came from within the educational world itself — from the nascent teaching profession, from ambitious and innovative urban school boards, from permanent officials within the Education Department and from new levels of parental expectation. More significant yet were the pressures bearing on the education system as a result of wider social and economic changes — from the progressive extension of the franchise; from the more confident demands of organized labour; from the perceived threat posed by powerful new international competitors; from calls across the political spectrum for a refocusing of 'national efficiency' and imperial leadership through collectivist agencies; from a new, more organic conception of the State's role most clearly seen in the writings of TH Green — from that constellation of change culminating in what George Dangerfield memorably understood as 'the strange death of Liberal England' (Dangerfield, 1935). With that death, questions about national education could be framed in new ways or at least with changed emphases. Writing in 1918, Michael Sadler could, for example, ask a stark question which, a generation earlier, would have raised liberal eyebrows

> What part can skilfully organized public education play in furthering
> the welfare and increasing the might of the modern State? (Sadler,
> 1918, p. 7)

In the life of that generation which straddled the turn of the century then, the very meaning of national education was being transformed. It is important to understand something of this cardinal moment, for in changing the scope of the education system itself, it also changed the implications of the mechanisms by which that system was supplied.

The fundamental drive of the change was to recast the idea of national education, moving it away from the nineteenth century principle of separate, self-contained and unrelated subsystems of schooling, towards the principle of a single national structure in which the subsystems were interlinked by channels along which individual pupils might move (Gordon *et al.*, 1991, p. 12). This was, in other words, a move away from a hierarchical view based on inherited privilege or disadvantage towards greater openness, based on social justice, the realization of individual ability and, of course, the rather differently conceived promotion of national efficiency. It was a move which was presaged some years before, in 1870, when WE Forster, introducing the first legislative provision for national education could declare that,

> . . . England for the future is in truth to be self-governed; all her
> citizens taking their share, not by class distinctions, but by individual
> worth. (Forster in Roach, 1991, p. 3)

It would be quite wrong to see this movement as being completed either intellectually or practically in the course of a single generation. It was not until

1944 that the idea could be expressed in the form of national legislation and not for a further twenty years that it could be expressed in its most developed form in the reorganization of secondary schooling along comprehensive lines. Nevertheless, in the years around the turn of the century the idea, in which these later reforms were immanent, began to penetrate popular and political consciousness to an extent which made adherence to the old nineteenth-century model of educational provision untenable. It was no longer a matter of whether the principles underlying national education should change, but rather of how rapidly change could be achieved in practice. The political battles of the twentieth century would be fought over the latter and not the former.

The Structure of Schooling in the Nineteenth Century

New conceptions of national education inevitably impinged on the issue of the mechanisms through which schooling should be delivered. In the nine-teenth century, as now, there were three principal potential sources of school-ing supply — private endeavour, charitable voluntary effort and provision by the State. These were however deployed in a very different relation than was to be the case in the twentieth century. We can get a clear idea of this if we glance at the educational landscape at mid-century, at the time of the unique Education Census of 1851.

The picture which emerges from the Census, though numerically uncer-tain, is structurally clear. The educational market was a highly differentiated one, divided into a sharply demarcated series of concentric sectors, access to which was limited by income and therefore by social class. These sectors were identified by contemporaries in the unambiguous language of an age in which social mobility was rare and in which the discourses of democracy and still less of meritocracy had limited purchase; schools were grouped as being 'superior', 'middling' and 'inferior' — catering respectively for upper, middle and working-classes (1851 Education Census, p. xxxiii; these categorizations were also widely used in the enquiries of local statistical societies in the 1830s and 1840s). A key distinction between the first two categories and the third was the degree to which they were privately controlled — responsible, in other words, to the demands of fee-payers and to no public authority. In the case of the 'middling' sector, elements of such control were to be retained in some degree until the passage of the 1944 Act. For the 'superior' sector, that control remains substantially in place, as it did in the mid-nineteenth century. The failure to incorporate such schools into the public sector in the post-war educational settlement remains, for many, its most damaging feature (see A.H. Halsey quoted in *Education Guardian*, 18 January, 1994, p. 3).

The pattern of the 'inferior' sector — accommodating almost 90 per cent of the school population in the nineteenth century — was complex (Hurt, 1979, p. 5). A common assumption of educational writers and observers in the nineteenth century was that the working-class were essentially incapable of generating much in the way of educational demand, still less of independent educational provision (Gardner, 1984). To the degree that schooling for this class was seen as desirable, it would therefore have to be provided through an external agency. This assumption has subsequently been incorporated into most liberal historical interpretations. These have characteristically charted the progressive development of popular schooling exclusively as the result of the agency of enlightened public authority — specifically that of the established church and the State. This interpretation has much strength, particularly for the closing decades of the century, but at mid-century, it does not fit so well. This is because, unexpectedly, there was then a large presence of private schools in the 'inferior' sector. Just as 'middling' and 'superior' social groups had access to independent schools under their direct financial control, so too did substantial elements of the working class (Laqueur, 1976). The fees of these working-class private schools were calculated in pence rather than guineas. They were mostly of modest or poor educational quality. The quality of the schools is however a less significant issue than the fact of their very existence, and how this might best be understood.

The major problem in explaining working-class private schools in the nineteenth century — it was certainly a problem which taxed the early HMIs — was why they should exist at all when the 'inferior' sector contained many other schools of apparently better quality and demonstrably lower financial cost to users. This alternative supply comprised schools which were supplied by the joint efforts of the State and the churches. The first mainstream elementary schools to be fully financed from public funds did not appear until after the 1870 Act, which inaugurated locally elected education authorities — the school boards. For Britain, this represented, by comparison with continental neighbours, a relatively late entry into national system-building in education. The reasons for this had historical roots both wide and deep. Until the 1870s, pervasive distrust of state involvement in civil society was shared by most shades of political opinion. Such distrust was very complex, rooted in memories of the 'Old Corruption' of the eighteenth century, in non-conformist suspicions of the established Church, in strong local traditions of voluntary association and in the celebration of the freedoms of the 'Free-born Englishman' against the perceived servitude of continental despotisms. This general constellation of distrust for central government was, in terms of the development of national education, augmented by the pervasive 'religious problem' of the nineteenth century — the inability of the State to take decisive legislative action for fear, by turns, of alienating Church or dissent (Cruikshank, 1963). Nevertheless, one of the real 'peculiarities of the English' — an overworked phrase — was that the principle of limited state intervention on pragmatic grounds was also widely and willingly accepted — not least by classical political economy (Green, 1990, Thane in Thompson, 1990). Thus it was that when it came, in 1833, the entry of the State into the provision of elementary schooling took the form not of direct initiative, but of public subsidy to the existing schools of the national religious societies. In much modified form, public financial support for non-provided schools has from that point remained an important feature of British national education.

How was it that working-class private schools could retain any place in the 'inferior' sector against the subsidized church schools? The answer seems to lie in the different degree of control which users could exert over each type. Church schools were often seen as excessively morally intrusive and overbearing in terms of the regulation of behaviour and attendance (Gardner, 1984). Private schools were more responsive to the vicissitudes of parental demand.

> In these schools, the teachers have no authority to consult, they have no one else to please . . . their faults and their merits alike arise from a desire to meet the exact demands which the parents make. (PP, 1870 LIV, p. 54)

Working-class users found that these schools responded to their demands in much the same way as the 'middling' and 'superior' schools responded to the different demands of their own distinctive constituencies. In this respect, it is important to note that the voluntary church schools were perceived by users and educational commentators alike as 'public' schools. The assertion of free market revisionists such as EG West that, because they were merely aided by, and not directly supplied by, the State, these schools can fairly be claimed as 'private' would certainly have jarred with nineteenth-century users if not suppliers (West, 1975, p. 78).

From Private to Public

The working-class private school was a ubiquitous presence in the mid-nineteenth century urban environment. Thirty years later, it was all but extinct. By the turn of the century it was forgotten. What happened? Why did such schools disappear? The answers to this question have a significance which goes beyond the fate of the schools themselves. The answers give us some clues as to the character of more general changes, both long-term and short-term, which were to affect the entire structure of national educational provision.

In the long-term, the fate of the working-class private school helps us to see how an educational system dominated by market supply could move to a system dominated by central provision and regulation. In the nineteenth century, privately-supplied schooling effectively constituted a continuum supplying the bulk of the nation's educational demand. One way of understanding the nature of educational change from the 1830s onwards is as the progressive engagement of the State with this continuum. First to be engaged were working-class private schools, because the formation and regulation of popular education were generally seen to constitute the leading and most pressing problem of policy in national education. The commitment of public funds to the problem on a scale that would have amazed early nineteenth-century opinion was now accepted, if sometimes grudgingly. A result was that the quality, range and potential of publicly-funded schooling increased rapidly. The gap between the quality of private and public provision, once much narrower, became so great that the inadequacies of private schooling could be recognized as intolerable. For users of elementary schools, a trade-off in terms of control over their own schools in favour of the advantages of better education and lower costs became increasingly attractive. At the same time as demand was changing in this way, the supply of traditional private schools was itself beginning to fall away. In part, this was due to the improv-ing quality of public education, but more immediately significant was the appearance at local level of school boards anxious to do what they could to hasten the demise of a form of schooling which was perceived to be out of date and inefficient (Gardner, 1992). The result of these combined changes was that the long tail of the nineteenth-century private school continuum dis-appeared very rapidly in the 1870s and 1880s. From this point on, the educa-tion of the working-class would take place entirely within the public arena, through schools either supplied or subsidized by the State.

The resolution of the problem of popular schooling in this way satisfied the proposition that the working class were either incapable of providing their own education, or that it was inappropriate for them to do so. Its less ex-pected effect was to compromise the next sector in the private school con-tinuum — in the old terminology, that of the 'middling' schools. After the 1870 Act, the momentum of elementary education pushed ahead rapidly, stimu-lated by increased public spending and by the collective energy and enthusi-asm of many of the new urban school boards. As a result the quality of lower middle-class schooling was progressively exposed as relatively poor. From the 1880s, and particularly in localities where school boards began to flirt with quasi-secondary schooling in the form of higher-grade schools, the lower middle-class began to desert their private schools and to throw in their lot with publicly-provided schooling. This absorption of elements of the middle-class into the public sector was a long, complex and often bitter process. For many, the prospect of their children sitting alongside the children of the working-class in provided schools was a savage blow in terms of social status. Those who could not tolerate incorporation in this way clung to the numer-ous suburban private villa schools — generally of very modest quality — which continued to offer a safe alternative to the board schools, or council schools as they became after the Act of 1902. Private schools of this character continued to find a considerable market — especially for female pupils — throughout the inter-war years.

Rapidly increasing public spending on elementary schooling after 1870 was much commented upon by contemporaries. Writing just before the out-break of the First World War, Henry Craik observed that,

In no sphere of activity has the advance of State intervention, after
centuries which saw very little but voluntary effort, been so astonishing . . . It is often overlooked that effective State intervention began
only about eighty years ago . . . marvellous advances have been made
at a cost that would have aroused the alarm of our fathers and
grandfathers . . . (Craik, 1914, p. vii)

Against this background, it was clear that patterns of social distinction through
education could only be maintained if middle-class education — comprising
a broad and diverse band of secondary schools arranged beneath the shadow
of the elite public schools — was also publicly supported in some fashion. The
middle-class, in the words of Lord Carlingford, 'did not find itself subject to
the paternal care of the State, either in the matter of favour or chastisement.'
(Gardner, 1984, p. 210). The voices of penurious middle-class parents seeking
to educate their children unaided were increasingly heard, making much the
same observation. These were appeals which chimed with the growing anxiety of central government to reorganize secondary schooling in the same
systematic way in which the elementary sector was being reformed. In the
provision of secondary education then, the State and the middle-class constituency for such schools shared a common goal. This was the creation of a
body of efficient schools supported in part by public funds, but continuing
to charge a level of fees safeguarding a significant level of user control and
ensuring continued social exclusivity.

In part such a goal was met by the incremental reorganization of ancient
charitable foundations following the Endowed Schools Act of 1869 (Roach,
op. cit., Part I). More immediately significant was the impact of the 1902 Act,
which gave powers to the newly constituted local education authorities for the
local provision of secondary as well as elementary schooling — powers which
had been denied to the old school boards. Supported by public funds, the new
municipal grammar schools could clearly be conceived as elements within a
developing picture of systematic national provision. But through the reten-
tion of fees, that social exclusivity which middle-class parents had previously
associated with the private sector, could also be preserved. Though this exclusivity was successfully defended throughout the inter-war years, it became
progressively harder to do so. The price for public subsidy had ultimately to
be paid by the middle-class parent, as in different circumstances and with
different consequences, it had earlier been paid by the working-class parent.
The image of places at secondary schools provided by public agency being
allocated on the basis of wealth and market power rather than ability was
increasingly challenged, particularly after the publication of Tawney's influential 'Secondary Education for All' in 1922. This critique of unequal access to
secondary schooling caught the mood of changing national perceptions of
what national education should represent. In 1907, regulations implemented
by the Liberal government had already signalled a response to this change in

opening a channel between elementary and secondary sectors (Sanderson, 1987, p. 24). Henceforth, up to 25 per cent of places in the grammar schools were required to be free. Though many of these scholarship places were in fact filled by the children of middle-class parents, the principle of meritocratic access to secondary schooling had moved onto the public agenda. The principle was strikingly implemented in the Act of 1944 which, in removing fees from publicly supplied secondary schooling, ended the guaranteed access of middle-class children to the local grammar school. For many middle-class parents, there was the anguish — unimagined by their own parents — of scholarship failure for their children, with no prospect of buying an acceptable alternative in the market for private education which, since 1902, had been in contraction.

In the long-term — from the entry of the State into educational provision in 1833, to its dramatic guarantee of secondary schooling for all in 1944 — we can see the incremental shift from a prospect of national education based on the operation of a segregated market place to one based on the guarantee of the State to equal access to schooling provided by public agency for all. As it progressed, this movement bore on each social class at different times and in different ways, but by 1944, few groups remained who had been untouched or unaffected by its long trajectory over more than a century.

Public Schooling and Public Opinion

If we return to the disappearance of working-class private schooling in the late nineteenth century, we can now see it as one episode in a larger story in which the market, the State and social class have been entangled over many generations. But this episode also has a short-term dimension which too is informative. It tells us how, in the space of a single generation, a great swathe of public opinion could begin to transfer its loyalty to — or perhaps more accurately, suspend its distrust of — a system of schooling that was supplied through the agency of the State rather than through a market attuned to popular demand (Briggs, 1984, p. 2).

One of the most striking features of the years following the passing of the 1870 Act was the degree to which, through the new board schools and the work of their associated school-attendance officers, the agency of the State came to be seen by working-class users as the legitimate, indeed the natural, supplier of popular schooling. This was a strange, flawed but ultimately genuine loyalty, in which important residual elements of earlier market principles for a time overlapped the new principle of public provision. An illustration of this is the widespread popular attachment to fee-paying. Though universal compulsion was introduced in 1880, schooling was not made free. This anomaly did not lead to great popular opposition on grounds of principle, though for some years police courts overflowed with the parents of recidivist non-attenders (Rubinstein, 1969). For most, the payment of notional fees was perceived as maintaining a token of independence in a system in which schools were now provided or extensively aided by public finance. The last fees in public elementary schools were not abolished until the 1918 Education Act; there are many alive today who remember arriving at school clutching their weekly school pence. But even after 1918 there were many older citizens for whom the association of free educational provision with 'charity' continued to linger (Parsons, 1978, p. 76).

In its formative period, popular loyalty to provided schooling was then ambivalent in character, drawing much inspiration from the developing educational programme of the labour movement, but without entirely losing an older radical suspicion of the State in general. Nevertheless, in the two generations which followed the 1870 Act, the British working-class put their faith in the agency of public authority in education in a way that no other social grouping would subsequently match. This was a faith rooted more in hope for the future rather than belief in the present. The British working-class began to see public education not in the defensive terms which had, a generation before, informed their adherence to their own private schools. Instead, public schooling could take on the positive promise of a better and more equitable life for the generation to come. In practice, parents could remain suspicious of the public elementary schools and their teachers; they seldom if ever, visited their children's schools (Parsons, 1978, pp. 107, 121, 130). Yet, by the turn of the century, it was to the State that the working-class would henceforth look for the provision of its schools as part of a national system in which the fulfilment of individual opportunity for all seemed ultimately possible. From the defence of their sectional interest through private schooling as the best to be expected in an unequal and unjust society, the bulk of the working population moved to a nobler, if much more risky, allegiance to the promise of a democratic national system of education asking and offering the best to all its citizens. The degree to which the subsequent course of twentieth-century educational history has repaid this allegiance is a matter for debate. Just over a century ago, the 1888 Royal Commission on the Elementary Education Acts called before it as a witness 'A Representative of the Working-Classes', Thomas Smyth, a plasterer by trade. His evidence signals an ambition, then still novel, which retains its force and its vision, if now, three generations later, tempered by pathos and the wisdom of experience.

> I believe that the State ought to find all and every requirement of . . . education . . . My contention is that we ought not to provide education for any class specially, but that all the educational facilities ought to be equal and open to all classes. (Smyth in Gardner, 1991, p. 169)

References

BRIGGS, A. (1984) 'Towards the welfare state', in BARKER, P. (Ed) *Founders of the Welfare State*, London, Heinemann.

CRAIK, H. (1914) 3rd ed *The State in its Relation to Education*, London, Macmillan.

CRUICKSHANK, M. (1963) *Church and State in English Education*, London, Macmillan.

DANGERFIELD, G. (1935) *The Strange Death of Liberal England*, London, Constable.

GARDNER, P. (1984) *The Lost Elementary Schools of Victorian England,* London, Croom Helm.

GARDNER, P. (1991) ' "Our schools; their schools". The case of Eliza Duckworth and John Stevenson', *History of Education*, 20, pp. 163–186.

GARDNER, P. (1992) 'Liverpool and the recognised non-certified efficient elementary private adventure school', *Journal of Educational Administration and History*, 124, pp. 186–96.

GORDON, P., ALDRICH, R. and DEAN, D. (1991) *Education and Policy in England in the Twentieth Century*, London, Woburn.

GREEN, A. (1990) *Education and State Formation: The Rise of Education Systems in England, France and the USA*, London, Macmillan.

HURT, J.S. (1979) *Elementary Education and the Working Classes*, London, RKP.

KINGSTON, P. '1944 and all that' in *Education Guardian*, 18 January 1994, p. 3.

LAQUEUR, T. (1976) 'Working class demand and the growth of English elementary education' in STONE, L. (Ed) *Schooling and Society*, Baltimore, Johns Hopkins University, pp. 192–205.

PARSONS, C. (1978) *Schools in an Urban Community: A Study of Carbrook 1870–1965*, London, RKP.

PP 1852–53 XC 1 'Education Census of Great Britain 1851'.

PP 1870 LIV 'Schools for the Poorer Classes in Birmingham, Leeds, Liverpool and Manchester'.

ROACH, J. (1991) *Secondary Education in England 1870–1902*, London, Routledge.

RUBINSTEIN, D. (1969) *School Attendance in London 1870–1904*, Hull, University of Hull.

SADLER, M. (1918) 'Introduction', in Friedel, V.H. *The German School as a War Nursery*, London, Andrew Melrose.

SANDERSON, M. (1987) *Educational Opportunity and Social Change in England,* London, Faber and Faber.

SUTHERLAND, G. (1971) *Elementary Education in the Nineteenth Century*, London, Historical Association.

THANE, P. (1990) 'Government and society in England and Wales 1750–1914', in THOMPSON, F.M.L. (Ed) *The Cambridge Social History of Britain 1750–1950*, Cambridge, CUP, vol 3, pp. 1–61.

WARDLE, D. (1974) *The Rise of the Schooled Society*, London, RKP.

WEST, E.G. (1975) *Education and the Industrial Revolution in England and Wales*, London, Batsford.

Part 1

Examining Particular Applications of the Market Principles in Practice

Chapter 3

Local Education Authorities and the Market Place

Geoff Morris

> Marketing is the idea or concept that an organisation's decisions should be governed by its market and its customers rather than by its technical facilities. (Hannagan, 1992, p. 15, para., 1.9)

Local education authorities (LEAs) used to be monopoly providers of publicly funded non-higher education and related services. At the heart of the 1944 Education Act was the three-way partnership between central government, which was responsible for national policy and strategy and for monitoring the LEAs; the LEAs which were charged with the responsibility of providing the schools, securing the provision of further education and employing the teachers and support staff; and the institutions themselves. The role assigned to the LEAs was reinforced by the requirement to maintain the church schools so that, with the exception of the capital costs of the voluntary sector, the LEAs had a monopoly in the provision of educational facilities and employed all those engaged at local level in the education service except staff in the voluntary aided schools. Fifty years later LEAs find themselves fighting for survival in the market place, and no-one but a supreme optimist would forecast a significant role for them in the future. How and why has this happened and does the market place offer them any hope?

Those who run monopolies tend to develop a mind-set to match, even, or perhaps especially, when the monopoly has been established by law. It was perhaps inevitable that a number of LEAs developed over the years a degree of inflexibility, not to say arrogance, which was largely unnoticed by themselves but plainly visible to others, notably the consumers of their services. The permissive 1960s have become synonymous in the eyes of the New Right with 'trendiness' in teaching content and methodology, but the decade also saw the birth of the consumer movement which for consumers in general found expression in the establishment of the Consumers' Association and the publication of *Which?* magazine, and in the education context led to the foundation of the Campaign for the Advancement of State Education and the Advisory Centre for Education. Perhaps as a result of a better educated generation of parents, the consumers of education became more discerning and critical, the public more demanding, and, as a consequence, the politicians began to take more interest in the subject than ever before. LEAs, on the whole, acted defensively to these developments. They, after all, were the democratically elected bodies charged with the duty of providing and staffing the schools and having responsibility for what went on in them. They were guided by professional officers and expert advisers and took pride in the way they did things, and most had a genuine interest and belief in the quality of the services they provided. So they reacted in the same way that any public body or group of professionals would have done thirty years ago when challenged by laymen or 'amateurs', and although it is easy with hindsight to see how education was provider-led rather than consumer-led these attitudes were common at the time and by no means confined to the education service.

But however much the LEAs and the education 'Establishment' generally defended their corner, the critical interest of ever more demanding parents refused to go away, and in 1976 the Prime Minister himself delivered what was to be the key-note speech for the following decade when he criticized standards of achievement in schools and invited a 'Great Debate' on what was to be done to halt the decline. The speech coincided with the publication of a report of an enquiry into the teaching and management of the William Tyndale school in London, following complaints by the largely working-class parents that their children were failing to learn adequately. The LEA as well as the school was criticized: '. . . if insufficient or unsuitable education is being provided at the school, or if insufficient regard is being paid to the wishes of parents of pupils in the school, the authority must do something about it (Auld, 1976, p. 270, para., 828). And so a climate was fostered in which the public, encouraged by the media, became increasingly critical of the quality of the education service, and the politicians, never slow to spot a vote-winning mood, gradually stepped up their attacks on teachers, teacher trainers, and, above all, on the LEAs which were cast in the role of arch-villains. Not only were the LEAs perceived as extravagant, arrogant and ignorant of what was happening to the quality of education in their schools, but often as 'loony' by the rightist press and politicians, who used some of the dottier manifestations of equal-opportunity policies, for example, to castigate and smear by association local education authorities generally. Thus the scene was set for the Thatcher revolution which introduced into the education service the philosophy and practice of the market, and strove to emasculate the LEAs with their interventionist and paternalistic approach, and their politically incorrect stance in the eyes of the government.

During the first Thatcher administration the government had more pressing matters on its agenda than education, but their intentions were signalled in legislation aimed at increasing the voting power of parents and decreasing that of LEA representatives on the governing bodies of schools, and in the increasing emphasis in speeches and statements of the importance of parents and of choice. As the 1980s progressed, Conservative thinking developed along these lines: standards are too low, and we cannot trust the teachers with their trendy notions or the LEAs with their ponderous bureaucracies and idiosyncratic priorities to do anything about raising them. We will therefore transfer the key levers of power away from the LEAs to central government, and legislate to expose standards achieved in schools whilst making them more accountable. At the same time we will give parents maximum opportunity to exercise choice, thus replicating conditions in the market place. Ironically the idea of delegating management responsibility, particularly financial responsibility to schools had been the brainchild of a handful of LEAs in the early 1980s. Like the government's later initiative the motives of these pioneers had been to raise educational standards. The argument articulated by one authority was:

> The idea was attractive managerially and politically (there was a broad consensus along the parties), while for the educationists there was the prospect that the power to manage their financial resources would give schools the ability to change direction in curriculum terms . . . If we could devise a workable system for delegating financial responsibility to schools . . . it might allow them to bring a greater degree of accuracy to their academic planning and to respond quickly to the need for curriculum change. (Morris, 1986, pp. 43–4)

The concept of local financial management (LFM) was simply based on the principle of good management that responsibility for spending should rest with those who will directly experience the consequences of that spending. It had nothing to do with free market economics and assumed a continuing key role for the LEA as employer, provider of support services, planner of the network of schools and monitor of their quality. Kenneth Baker on a visit to schools in Peterborough as Secretary of State on 1 October 1986 discovered at first-hand how the LFM scheme operated in Cambridgeshire at that time, and in the following weeks made a number of references to the benefits of this 'new' idea and the important place it would have in his party's manifesto for the coming election.

The 1988 Education Act translated Conservative thinking on education into a legislative framework within which a market place approach could operate as freely as possible within a public education service. For the first time in our history a national curriculum was prescribed by law, which established a core curriculum of maths, English and science and a six-subject foundation curriculum together with compulsory religious education. Attainment targets were introduced and pupils were to be tested at the ages of 7,11,14, and 16. There was thus a standard 'product' available in the education market place and a control system intended to guide the parent-consumer towards those schools which delivered a quality product. In order to enable schools to improve their product it was necessary to give them freedom to manage their resources, so the provisions relating to local management of schools (LMS) formed an essential element in the Act. LMS went far beyond the early models developed by the LEAs. The technical details in the legislation and subsequent regulations were designed to eliminate any trace of discretion on the part of the LEAs or their officers in the way budgets were distributed, and prescribed a formula approach for all monies which were to form part of schools' delegated budgets. Although these formulae could vary from one LEA to another, they were monitored in rigorous detail by the DES. The formulae were geared to the number and ages of the pupils: the more pupils the larger the budget; the larger the budget the more scope a school had to improve its curriculum range and its facilities. Increasingly the regulations have obliged LEAs to delegate a greater proportion of the overall budget for education to the schools, so that enormous pressure has been brought to bear on the budgets for the administration and centrally provided support services of the LEA. The Act also gave the governing bodies the *de facto* powers of employers, even though the legal responsibility for employment matters remained with the LEA — a distinct whiff of power without responsibility — so that the key resource of the school was also removed from LEAs and managed at school level.

Finally, choice for the parents was to be enhanced. Hitherto, LEAs had managed admissions to schools under the provisions of the 1980 Education Act, designed to enable the problem of falling school rolls to be handled in a sensible way. The LEAs with their overview of demographic change and knowledge of school capacities, were empowered to fix limits to the number of pupils to be admitted to individual schools and to determine criteria for admission. This enabled the authorities to maintain enough schools to cope with anticipated pupil numbers, predicted to increase in the future, and to plan meanwhile for any necessary school closures or mergers to be properly programmed to match fluctuating school rolls. In this way a viable network of schools covering the area could be maintained. As a consequence however, many schools had admission limits well below their physical capacity, and inevitably a number of parents were disappointed at not getting their first choice. This kind of sensible planning and management of the system was anathema to the market place protagonists, and the antithesis of the political thinking behind the 1988 Education Act, and was duly eliminated. The Act provided that a school can admit as many pupils as it wishes up to its 'standard number', effectively the physical capacity of the buildings. How much the legislation delivers real choice, rather than simply satisfying government rhetoric, is highly questionable, but parental choice nevertheless provides the third pillar on which government strategy rests. Parents are in the market place as consumers (pupils as consumers do not rate a mention); the schools provide a standard product (at least as far as the national curriculum is concerned) with varying degrees of success, and have freedom to manage their resources as they wish; the better the quality of the school (measured by published tables) the more popular it will be, and consequently the greater its budget. In the same way the unsuccessful school will go to the wall. The ultimate choice placed in the hands of parents is whether they wish their school to retain any connection at all with the LEA, or whether they prefer to 'opt out' and seek grant maintained status. This is reinforced in the 1993 Education Act which makes it easier and quicker for a school to become grant maintained. A further market pressure is thus brought to bear on LEAs in their attempts to discharge their responsibilities for planning the school system. An additional complication introduced by the same Act is that the LEA would be obliged to share the planning function with the Funding Agency for Schools (FAS) if 10 per cent of schools in any sector (primary or secondary) opt out. The 'loony' end of the spectrum of Conservative free-market dogmatists has moved beyond this to advocate that new state schools should be put out to tender, so that existing schools in the private sector can bid for contracts to run them (Fallon, 1993).

LEAs are nothing if not pragmatic, and have reacted to finding themselves in the market place by trying to make the new system work. They had already been exposed to commercial competition in the mid-1980s through Compulsory Competitive Tendering (CCT) which obliged local authorities (not just LEAs) to put certain services out to public tender. The process of having to bid against outside competition to retain the provision of catering, cleaning and grounds maintenance proved to be a valuable learning experience and taught authorities not only how to analyse real costs, and how to work the trade-off between cost and quality, but also how to reorganize themselves internally. Which part of the organization was a client buyer and which a direct service seller needed to be clear, and the new skill of managing outside contractors or agents had to be learned, often painfully. A number of authorities, especially those who had anticipated the legislation, had their fingers burned in early schemes because the private contractors were also having to acquire new knowledge. They were discovering, for example, that cleaning a school was a very different proposition from cleaning an office: a community school could not be cleaned in the evening; the floor of an infants' classroom needed more time than that of a sixth-form seminar room since the users spent a large part of their time sitting on it, spilling sand and water, and generally treating it in an un-office-like way. Moreover the cleaners were used to being treated as part of the school 'family' and resented the impersonal hard-headed management style that the outsiders often brought in. Providing catering services in large urban schools was relatively straightforward for the large catering companies, but most saw no future in trying to make a profit selling meals in a rural area with some hundreds of small schools, many in remote locations. It was therefore not surprising that most LEAs found themselves winning contracts for these support services, though this was seldom achieved without radical restructuring of the workforce and the painful process of redundancy.

Nevertheless, this early induction into the market-place was relatively easy, at least in conceptual terms. It could be legitimately argued that LEAs should not be misdirecting their energy and resources towards such things as cleaning and catering which were not central to the education process, and that hiving them off either to outside firms or to a discrete or 'arms-length' part of the authority made sense. However, education legislation of the late 1980s and early 1990s posed problems of a different philosophical order, since the new market place questioned the purposes and whole *raison d'être* of the LEA itself. As an ever-increasing proportion of the budget was delegated to schools it transferred buying-power to them and has forced LEAs to market and sell the kinds of professional services that were central to their very existence. The way schools choose to spend their money can now have a significant impact not only on the shape and organization of an authority's services, but also on the jobs and careers of many LEA staff. This has not only prompted the reorganization of LEA teams but has resulted in the creation of a new service ethic (*TES*, 1993). Although traditional values remain (stewardship of public resources, financial probity, public service, fair and equitable administration in order to ensure that the needs of all pupils are met), there is no doubt that a new culture has emerged in which the financial viability or marketability of a service or a support team has become a very important, perhaps even the most important, consideration.

Most authorities have now reorganized their various support teams on an agency basis in order to meet the demands of the market place. These, in simple terms, are that schools must be satisfied that a valued service is being provided at an affordable price, otherwise that service ceases to exist. The agencies work on a self-financing basis, and market their services not only to schools (including grant maintained schools) but also to the authority itself in the case of certain activities such as finance, personnel, or information technology. The size and number of the agencies varies: Buckinghamshire, for example, has a portfolio of forty-four services on offer and devolves 97 per cent of its budget to schools. One of its senior education officers puts the LEA's thinking like this:

> It enables schools to get the service they want, and it makes the service providers think long and hard about what their customers want and therefore about quality. On the other hand there are risks to things like the county music service if the level of buy-back cannot be sustained to provide the level of expertise that is needed. (Ecclestone, 1993)

Cambridgeshire with eighteen agencies has already experienced the effect of these risks with two agencies having been disbanded, but the authority still remains confident about the future:

> Everyone thought, when we took this initiative three years ago, that we had gone down suicide road. They thought we were going to lose vast amounts of custom. That has not happened. Our agencies have been very successful, but they have had to work very hard, be more responsive and improve efficiency. (Gale, ibid., 1993)

In that authority the personnel agency has become an entirely private organization, freed from the restrictions of local government legislation and marketing its services beyond the boundaries of the county. Another, the school support agency, now sells its services exclusively to the LEA because the schools valued it so much that they preferred not to have that element of the budget delegated and be exposed to the vagaries of the market. Other LEAs have chosen to offer a 'table d'hôte' menu rather than 'à la carte': schools may choose to buy into a 'mega-agency' providing many different services, and if they choose not to do so must look elsewhere (a hint of blackmail here!). Local authority inspection teams provide another illustration of the way in which the market place is impacting on professional services. The establishment of the Office for Standards in Education (OFSTED), and the requirement that the four yearly inspections of schools be carried out by a team selected as a result of competitive tendering, has thrown this hitherto purely professional branch of the 'education establishment' into the hurly-burly of the commercial world. A large proportion of registered inspectors are LEA inspectors/advisers and these now find themselves directly involved in cost/quality judgments, business planning and contract bidding. At the same time they are having to maintain their former role as monitors of the quality of schools in their own LEAs, and it remains to be seen how long this dual role can be sustained as the programme of inspections gets under way. Certainly the experience of a number of front runners in the agency business is that the buying of LEA support services works best if there is one dominant buyer (i.e., LEA or schools) rather than an equality in demand.

The education market place, and consequent development of agencies, has affected relationships not only between schools and LEA but also within Town and County Halls. Education departments were the first to feel the tensions that a commercial ethos brings to organizations accustomed to a collegiate way of working. If, for example, a school wants advice about a personnel matter, and initially brings its problem to a member of the school-support agency, does that officer deal with it and charge for the service, or should it be referred to the real experts in the personnel agency which would then take the fee and enhance its income? Or, to take another method of service pricing, a school telephones an education officer to discuss an important and urgent matter, but has not bought-in to that service. Does that officer refuse to deal with it on the grounds that the school has not paid its 'subscription' or will professional conscience prevail? Colleagues, accustomed to co-operative team working, are in danger of becoming competitors within the same organization. Each authority is having to resolve these difficulties: many have done so, others are just beginning to face them, but whatever *modus operandi* is worked out, the market ethic now has a place alongside traditional professional codes within the culture of the LEA.

Other departments were slower to react. It took some time for the message of the 1988 Act to reach lawyers, treasurers and property officers that they too were in the market place, not only in relation to the schools but also in relation to the education department, which now had a keen incentive to identify, and if possible reduce, the costs of the 'central' departments on its own budget. Traditionally the education department carried a figure in its budget of the overall cost of central services which related to the size of the education budget in relation to that of the council as a whole. Post-1988 chief education officers saw themselves as buyers of these services, pressed for their funding to be delegated to them in exactly the same way that the education budget was largely delegated to schools, and set about trying to negotiate cheaper rates or to reduce costs by looking elsewhere. Central departments in turn set up agencies as they realized that reduced demand from the education service could bring about corresponding reductions in the size of their own operations. When an education department finds itself in the role of both buyer and seller of services it is hard to escape the conclusion that the LEA's decisions are increasingly being governed by the market.

At the same time, there have been important positive developments emerging from the new commercialism. Attitudes towards the users and clients of LEA services have been revolutionized. Although the shrill rhetoric of the New Right about LEAs being the self-interested bureaucratic oppressors of the schools must be kept in proper perspective, there was enough germ of truth in their polemics about attitudes to make all the more remarkable the sea-change in the way the providers of services now regard their clients. A customer-friendly approach has replaced management by control, and the assumption that the provider always knows best. LEAs have seen the importance of researching the needs of their clients carefully, indeed compulsory competitive tendering (CCT) has forced them to do this, and from determining needs it is possible to identify what functions must be performed, as Cordingley and Kogan have pointed out (Cordingley and Kogan, 1993, chapters 6 and 7). The spending power of schools has clarified wonderfully what it is they need from outside the institution itself in order to discharge their functions, and this in turn is enabling them to help define and shape the kind of LEA they want. This can not happen without dialogue, and the creation of a process to enable heads and governors to contribute to the development of authority policies and strategies. A number of authorities, identifying the schools as 'stake-holders' in the authority itself, have set up mechanisms to enable the aspirations of the stake-holders to be articulated. These have sometimes been designed to be at arms-length from the authority, such as the Leeds Schools' Commission with its formal constitution, independent chairmanship and representatives of the community, as well as heads and governors; sometimes they have been less formally structured, such as the Support Services Board in Cheshire, but in all cases the intention has been to provide a forum to enable the authority to listen to the views of schools about the nature and style of the LEA and the kind of support it should be providing for them. Perhaps equally importantly, these groups have promoted a new working partnership; one chief education officer has written: 'I have come to recognise the value of their deliberations as a starting point of a new relationship with schools, and as a clear pointer for me to the issues which are of pressing concern to Heads and Governors in this city.' (Strong, 1993)

Elsewhere, LEAs have relied on professional market research to provide objective data about client perceptions. Humberside, for example, commissioned a market survey company to identify the future buying intentions of schools prior to the delegation of additional budget heads, and at the same time provided workshops for LEA staff to help them 'develop the culture and skills associated with working in a commercial context associated with market research and service agreements.' (Garnett, 1993) The data provided by this survey revealed that awareness of the culture of a competitive market and the potency of market forces had 'permeated the educational field at the level of individual schools', and that heads would 'expect a quality service to be delivered, by personnel of proven ability in a climate which is sympathetic to client needs.' (ibid.)

One conclusion of the Humberside survey was that most respondents felt that they would neither need nor expect to look further than the LEA to provide them with the quality of service which they would want for their school. Despite the necessity of having to adopt the strategies and devices of the business world, and despite the freedom of choice now available to the purchasers, there is very little evidence that commercial suppliers are making any significant inroads into the traditional LEA services market. What success has been achieved has been largely by education consultants, most of whom have been former professionals in the education service, or by companies which have grown out of specialist branches of LEAs. It may be that there are not yet enough private suppliers of the specialist services required by schools, or it may be simply that heads do not want the additional burden of launching into the technicalities of commercial tendering and learning the skills of managing outside agencies (*TES*, 1993). We have seen that even in the areas of cleaning and catering, the direct-service organizations of local authorities have won the lion's share of the contracts, and although it is early days to draw conclusions about the professional agencies, there appears to be a similar pattern emerging. In Cambridgeshire, for example, 90 per cent of primary and 80 per cent of secondary schools are buying into the agencies. Nor can it be said that government expectations over grant maintained schools have been met: the rate of schools opting out stubbornly refuses to accelerate: in August 1993 there were still twenty-six LEAs in which no schools had voted to opt out, and the fifty-one LEAs in which more than three schools had done so accounted for 93 per cent of the total. There is no evidence that grant maintained schools have had any significant impact on the choices parents and pupils make about schools. Moreover, they have provided 'no evidence that competition between schools contributes to any increase in standards.' (Fitz *et al.*, 1993)

The evidence, then, suggests that the market place environment has not yet brought private-sector entrepreneurs significantly into the education world, and if this was the intention then the policy has been a failure. Local authorities are, of course, at an advantage in their experience, expertise and established position in the field, and are able to provide services at cost without a profit-margin to consider. Even so, they have been obliged to reorganize and stream-line their operations, shed staff and undergo a major attitudinal change. The most positive benefits for LEAs have been the increased awareness of the need for efficiency, financial management of a high order, and a close-to-customer approach to the people they exist to serve, which demands accurate know-ledge of what schools and parents really need.

And yet the provision of support services is only one of the functions of an LEA, and, it can be argued, the least important. Provided schools are able to buy the kind of services they need of the right quality and at the right price, it does not much matter who supplies them. Certainly the case for a local, democratically elected body should not have to rely on the LEA role as a supplier of services. At least as important are two functions which do not easily fit into the market place philosophy: the support of individuals and the planning role. The first of these is concerned with the welfare of people whether they are children, with or without special educational needs, students needing advice about financial support for their higher education, or adults as learners or as parents. This is the area of entitlements, of equitable treatment, of individual grievances against the 'system', of the guardianship of the con-sumer interest, and is the very stuff of the traditional public service ethic of integrity and fairness. Some authorities see their role as purchaser of services for the whole community, acting as broker between the schools and parents, and monitoring the quality of performance in the services available. But the crucial role for the continuing significance of education as part of local gov-ernment is planning, and this is an area in which market forces have a very limited influence.

LEAs are essentially democratic decision-making bodies and their key role lies in formulating strategic policies and carrying them through. There has to be a set of democratic decisions about the pattern of schools in an area which need to be made by someone and kept under constant review. The decisions are about the number, location, size and shape of the schools; how the pupils get to these schools every day; what happens for those who need special education arrangements; what access should there be for adult learners and other users; how quality and safety management is to be monitored (Ferguson, 1993). Now these decisions could be placed in the hands of non-elected bodies (as the government is trying to engineer for decisions on plan-ning the pattern of school provision through the Funding Agency for Schools (FAS)), or the democratic process could be left simply to operate at national level, but such arrangements would be either logistically impossible, or would seriously impair public accountability, or both. The market does of course impact on these planning matters: parents vote to take schools out of LEA control, parental choice determines the viability of schools, but despite the drive to eliminate the need for planning, no effective substitute has yet been devised. Decisions about school closures and mergers, about provision for the under-fives, about how best to provide transport in particular local circumstances, about the level of community education to provide, must surely be based on local views, local knowledge and local needs, and be thrashed out in public debate by people who are directly accountable to local electors. There are those who are opposed to this kind of local democratic planning and decision-making, and who continue to advocate an unfettered market approach to this core activity of the LEA, but apart from its logistical impracticality, it is hard to see this being acceptable politically other than by extremist elements.

And this illustrates the difficulty facing the advocates of the free market in education. The whole thrust of the 1988 Act and subsequent legislation has been to loosen or break the links between schools and the LEA with the object of providing choice and promoting competition, and of emasculating the role and powers of the LEA. But there are too many impediments inherent in a state system of education to enable a free-market economy to work. In a free market, the aggregate of individual decisions to buy and sell will create adequate services and goods through the mechanism of supply and demand (Cordingley and Kogan, 1993, p. 98). A publicly provided national education service cannot work on that basis: there is no freedom to develop a new 'product' since the imposition of the national curriculum; the only choice available to the 'customer' is which 'outlet' to use, and this choice is constrained by location and capacity; the customers themselves are under legal compulsion, and the outlets are severely circumscribed in their freedom to choose which market sectors they will aim for. Financial inducements by government for schools to opt out absurdly contradict the whole rationale of the free market. Moreover, the money used in all these enterprises is public and cannot be used for personal gain or profit. If it were possible to close the failing school and to go on enlarging the successful one, as a supermarket might do with its various branches, it might be possible to realize the dream of the marketeers, but capital costs let alone location problems and time-scale rule this out as a practical proposition. And the national curriculum as the single product on offer provides yet another contradiction in the market approach. Parental choice is therefore a hoax. It seems unlikely that Conservative education thinkers have pondered the words of John Stuart Mill, who wrote in 1833:

> We may ask whether . . . the plan of nineteen-twentieths of our unendowed schools be not an organised system of charlatanerie for imposing on the ignorance of parents? Whether parents do, in point of fact, prove themselves as solicitous, and as well qualified to judge rightly of the merits of places of education as the theory of Adam Smith supposes? . . . Whether the necessity of keeping parents in good humour does not too often, instead of rendering education better render it worse? . . . (Mill, 1833, pp. 24–5)

It is evident that the market has had a significant impact on LEAs and has been a major factor in improving many of their policies, practices and attitudes. All authorities now have a consumer's eye view of the services they provide, and the old attitudes, once deeply ingrained in professionals, that they alone know what is best for the people they serve, have now disappeared. Enormous energy now goes into trying to discover what the client needs, and relationships between LEA officers and heads of schools are generally much improved. Management by contract and consent (where management still exists) have replaced management by control as the financial levers have been removed. Within the LEA, roles have been clarified, organization improved and flat structures have replaced steep hierarchies. The danger of the bottom line corrupting the public-service ethic is certainly present and keeping a balance will be crucial in the continuing development of authorities. Whether the local government review will, by reducing the size of LEAs below the point of viability, impair the more important functions of strategic decision-making in the policy and planning areas, in matching school places to pupils and in individual client support is not yet clear. Nevertheless it is hard to conceive of a future without a locally determined and accountable form of decision-making. Paradoxically, the legislation which aimed to sideline LEAs has created 25,000 pressure groups in the newly empowered governing bodies, which will undoubtedly demand more information and a greater input to national budget-making, and which will not tolerate remote and bureaucratic dictat from Whitehall replacing local accountable and accessible elected bodies. LEAs of the future may not be recognizable by past or present models, but political reality suggests that their core functions and culture will be vested in some form of locally accountable bodies whose decisions will take serious account of, but not be governed by, considerations of the market.

References

AULD, R. (1976) *William Tyndale Junior and Infant Schools Public Enquiry: a report to the ILEA*, London, Inner London Education Authority.

CORDINGLEY, P. and KOGAN, M. (1993) *In Support of Education: Governing the Reformed System*, London, Jessica Kingsley.

ECCLESTONE, T. and GALE, B. (1993) 'Heads pull the purse strings', *Times Educational Supplement*, 9 July 1993, p. 4.

FALLON, M. (1993) *Brighter Schools*, Social Market Foundation.

FERGUSON, J. (1993) 'The Governance of Education: the Decline and Re-emergence of the LEA,' Speech to Directors of Social Services (16.7.93).

FITZ, J., HALPIN, D. and POWER, S. (1993) *Grant Maintained Schools*, London, Kogan Page, p. 116.

GARNETT, M. (1993) 'Satisfaction guaranteed', *Education* (28.5.93), 181, 21, p. 411.

HANNAGAN, T.J. (1992) *Marketing for the Non-Profit Sector*, London, Macmillan.

MILL, J.S. (1833) 'The Right and Wrong of State interference with corporation and church property', in *Dissertations and Discussions*, London, Routledge.

MORRIS, G.H. (1986) 'The county LEA', in RANSON, S. and TOMLINSON, J. (Eds) *The Changing Government of Education*, London, Allen & Unwin.

STRONG, J. (1993) 'Strong riposte', *Letter in Education* (12.2.93) 181, 6, p. 116.

TIMES EDUCATIONAL SUPPLEMENT (*TES*), Agents for Change', 9 July 1993.

Chapter 4

In Defence of the Educational Voucher

Donald Naismith

The Development of Social Markets

One of the most significant social and political developments in recent years has been the introduction of market principles and practices into the provision of public services. One reason for this is the widening gap between what public services provide and the resources they need. As public services improve, higher expectations are put upon them constantly outstripping available resources, particularly if these are met from general taxation. There is a limit to what people are prepared or able to pay from their own pockets for universal benefits. But as individuals they are prepared to pay more to buy better services to which they attach particular importance than the State says it can afford. Parents are likely to be willing to pay more for a better education in the same way as higher investment in pensions may have a greater priority for middle-aged people.

One way to generate more resources to bridge the gap between rising expectations and relatively declining resources, is to increase personal choice between competing providers. Among additional important benefits would be sharper performance as a result of squeezing out restrictive practices inseparable from monopoly providers and the achievement of the higher national productivity the increasingly competitive world economy demands.

Consequently, the government has redefined its role. It no longer sees itself as the necessary sole provider of essential services, but as the guardian of the public interest through regulations controlling quality. The importance of this shift in the role of government cannot be underestimated. It is not merely a utilitarian question of practicality or organization. It raises the most fundamental issues about the nature of the individual and society and the relationship between the two. It is philosophical. Hence, reference is now frequently made to a 'social market' in which the methods of private enterprise are harnessed to social ends. No inherent conflict is seen between the pursuit of individual self-interest and the discharge of social responsibilities, nor is any automatic assumption made that social purposes can only be met through collective action. On the contrary. According to this line of argument the more government substitutes its opinion and behaviour for those of the individual, the more the individual is sucked into a dependency on the State and personal social responsibility is weakened.

The most basic needs which were once thought could or should be met only through collective action, for example health, energy, transport, water, housing and communications, have now been put on a more commercial basis. Neither central nor local government is immune from this process. Government is regarded by some as the cause of many social and economic problems rather than a solution. Re-inventing government is therefore firmly on the political agenda. Functions of government are being hived off to the private sector. Many of those remaining functions are being turned into free-standing, self-financing organizations.

Applying Social Market Principles to Education

Among the few major public services resistant to these fundamental changes is education. This is largely because there is confusion over who is the 'customer', the parent (or the child) or the State. Government reforms over the past decade, however, have brought the education system to a point where the creation of a social market in education is a distinct possibility. Three reforms are particularly important. First, the replacement of the monopolistic local education authority by the self-governing school competing for pupils and services as the basic building block in the system. Second, the great improvement in the quality of information about schools aimed at enabling parents to choose more appropriately. Third, the introduction of funding schools by formula in which the largest determinant is the number of pupils on roll. Related to this is the intended use of a common funding unit representing a national standard of cost of educating a pupil. This is the basis of a voucher; the essential dynamo of a demand-driven education system shaped by the needs and wishes of the user, not governed by those of the producer.

Although these three reforms could facilitate the creation of a demand-driven education system, they could, paradoxically, also lead to a more tightly organized supply-led system than we now have. It is easy to imagine the government going down the centralized route. The government already decides in great measure through the national curriculum what teachers should teach and how pupils should be assessed. It controls the examination system. The machinery to enable it to undertake responsibility for the supply of school places and the pattern of education in an area is already in place in the shape of the Funding Agency for Schools. It is only a short step to extend the grant maintained model to all schools to bring them under central government control. There is a strong likelihood that this will happen because it is the easiest course of action to take and there are well established, albeit obsolescent centralized systems, particularly in continental Europe with which ours is frequently and detrimentally compared. If this were to happen a unique opportunity would be missed to modernize our system which can only be achieved if the demand-driven model is adopted.

The demand-driven social market system would have the following four main features. First, all schools would become not only self-governing, but self-financing, receiving their income from parents not the State. Second, parents would be enabled to buy the education they wish for their children through being provided with a voucher representing a certain value to which they could add. By this means, money taken from the public through general taxation for education would be redirected to the parent. Third, the government would relinquish its planning role of trying to maintain a balance between the supply and demand of school places, and deciding whether schools should open, close or change their character. These matters would be largely left to the forces of parental demand within the framework of agreed national standards guaranteeing material provision and learning expectations. Fourth, the government would strengthen these quality-control mechanisms, in particular, efficient interventionist 'safety-net' arrangements to prevent schools which fall below acceptable standards continuing to operate.

Such a system would have very considerable advantages. Parents would have a greater involvement in the education of their children, a key element in the improvement of standards. It is unreasonable of the State to lay on parents a duty to educate their children, but to deny them the means to do so directly. The education service would become more efficient in financial as well as educational terms. Good schools would flourish, poor schools and unwanted places would be removed. A greater variety of kinds of schools more attuned to the differing needs of pupils would spring up: selective, academic, technological, denominational, creative-arts schools. Accountability would be strengthened. Local education authorities which cannot adequately represent parents' interests would give way to the parents' power to place their children in, or to remove them from, schools of their choice. Extra resources would find their way into the system as parents added to the value of their voucher. Unproductive bureaucracy would be removed, the damaging distinction between state schools and fee-paying schools eliminated. The blackmailing tactics of unions and the risk of government abuse of power would be prevented. There will always be disagreement, proper and sincerely held differences of opinion, about how children should be taught. It is surely preferable to allow such differences of educational vision to flourish. People can then choose from among them, subject, of course, to the safeguards only the State can provide. Above all, a dynamic force would enter the system bringing with it a responsiveness unachievable in a closed, planned system.

Arguments against and for Educational Vouchers

Opponents of such an approach will argue on two grounds: first, that it is inequitable; and second, that it is impractical. Giving everyone a voucher would subsidize the well-off and increase inequalities. It would be unfair. The scheme would be difficult, if not impossible, to implement. Vouchers would be lost, not claimed or misused. They could not cope with children moving from one school to another. Furthermore, there would need to be a new and a perhaps more complicated expensive bureaucracy.

The criticism that a voucher system would be inequitable may be met in the following ways. There is no reason why a voucher system should not be arranged in such a way as to benefit most the least well off. Vouchers could be means-tested perhaps as part of an increasingly consolidated system of tax-related social benefits. There could be an income level beyond which parents were not eligible to receive a voucher at all (i.e., they would have to purchase their child's education at their own expense). The technology necessary to the administration of such a system already exists. However, the most telling argument in favour of the voucher in terms of equity is simply that by financing the pupil rather than the institution, it provides a vehicle whereby the needs of each individual can more personally and accurately be met. It should be remembered how inequitable the present system is. There are wide variations in the quality of education in the state system and a growing independent sector. The knowing and the well-off can choose their school by deciding where to live and by paying for an education. Where is the equity in that?

The exercise of choice is first and foremost an ethical issue. Why should only the well-off choose? Practical considerations are secondary. The more fundamental fact of the matter is that planned systems are inherently incapable of providing education on a fair basis. Consider the track record of the most pure example of a planned system within our experience, that of the Inner London Education Authority and its predecessors. For over a hundred years here was a single-purpose authority, able to raise such money as it needed through precepts, foremost of its time under the same political control with all the levers of control at its disposal. If it had a *raison d'être* at all it was to transfer resources from the richer parts of inner London to the poorer. But in this it signally failed. In spite of many outstanding successes which deserve recognition it did not create an equitable system of education. There existed within its area not only as wide a variation in educational quality as in any part of the country, but some of the country's worst schools.

Self-evidently, a demand-driven system must be workable. It is hard to accept in our sophisticated society that the necessary administrative machinery cannot be devised to make a voucher system work. Vouchers are not only practicable because of their versatility they are the most efficient way of matching supply to demand and of meeting the changing needs of widely differing individuals. A voucher system could operate with the following characteristics. All eligible pupils would receive a voucher the value of which is decided by dividing the national budgetary allocation by the number of eligible people involved. As already mentioned, the value of the voucher may be restricted to certain income groups or be means-tested. In addition allowances or weightings could be introduced for special circumstances such as the extra help needed to cater for special needs. The voucher may belong to a separate transaction or be incorporated into the tax-benefit system. The value of the voucher may be increased to encourage attendance at certain studies in shortage subjects, for example, or weighted in the direction of particular aspects of the service: teacher training or adult-literacy programmes are instances. The fact that all eligible pupils receive a voucher would widen educational opportunities and increase take-up rates where attendance is voluntary. Not everyone outside compulsory education would use their vouchers immediately. Such vouchers may be 'saved' for future use. The value of the voucher may be indexed or left pegged at its initial value.

Vouchers would be accepted by all accredited institutions, whether fee-paying or free. Schools and colleges would recover the money from a government agency established for the purpose. For the beginning of every academic year each educational institution would make a decision on how many students can be accepted and set the tuition fee. A number of factors would need to be taken into account in setting the tuition fee such as the number of students likely to enrol and the cost of the education to be offered, exercises already familiar to further and higher education and the independent sector. Where the cost of the education exceeded the value of the voucher, the difference may be made up: this could be done in a variety of ways. It is accepted that a voucher system would need its own bureaucracy, but this would be less cumbersome than our burgeoning centralized system which brings with it by the month more rules and regulations, more legal challenges, greater inflexibility and a more pharisaical attitude to education.

The way to see whether a voucher system will work is to try it out on a pilot basis. Although vouchers are primarily associated with American educational thinking, increasing attention is being paid to the idea in Russia, which is radically restructuring its education system in the wake of the collapse of the soviet regime. There, interest is fuelled by the disintegration of the economy and the search for new ways to finance public services and by distrust, for obvious reasons, of centralized planned systems. One Russian region, Vladimir, has the federal government's permission to experiment with the introduction of vouchers from September 1994 in two of its school districts. The plan is that vouchers will initially be introduced to provide the financial basis for kindergarten education and for 'summer' schools and then be extended to supplementary courses and in-service teacher training before being applied to mainstream schooling.

One of the drawbacks of our system is that although new teaching methods can be introduced, seemingly at will, institutional change is difficult because we have no mechanism to allow experiments challenging the status quo to take place. The 'establishment' by its nature has no interest in encouraging alternatives. We lack the dynamism of the demand-driven system. It would be ironic if because of this we slide towards greater centralization and inflexibility whilst in Russia the seeds of a superior system are being sown. The Russian Minister of Education has described Russia as 'a laboratory for the world'. Our government should encourage experimentation here. It is no longer good enough to claim that vouchers are intellectually attractive but impracticable. The state of our education system requires us to have the courage to explore new ideas and ways of doing things. After all, that is what education is all about, surely?

Chapter 5

Diversity in State Education:
The Grant Maintained Option

Rosalie Clayton

> The Government believes that school autonomy and parental choice
> — combined with the National Curriculum — are the keys to achiev-
> ing higher standards in all schools. (Choice and Diversity: A New
> Framework for Schools, 1992)

A decade of ricocheting national debate about the quality of education cul-
minated eventually in a series of reforming Acts of Parliament which set out
a national strategy intended to enhance the quality of primary and secondary
education in England and Wales. As the 1992 White Paper 'Choice and Diversity' so succinctly summarizes, there are three cornerstones of this strategy.
The first is intended to standardize curriculum content, the second to put
schools in the market place and the third to give them the autonomy to
respond to market forces. However, at the same time the very nature of the
market itself had also to be transformed by the removal of monopolies and
the introduction of diversity and competition.

The aim was to raise standards. Education in our schools had, rightly or
wrongly, been judged a failure and the educational establishment — LEAs,
HMI, teacher-training institutions and schools — were no longer to be trusted
to achieve the goals identified while the status quo persisted. Open enrolment,
local management of schools (LMS) and grant maintained status (GMS) were
designed to shift the balance of power in such a way as to unfreeze the status
quo, creating a climate and momentum for change.

Transforming the Market Place

School autonomy or the self-governing school was an idea of the 1980s which
has the potential to influence the next few decades of British education. Since
the Butler Act of 1944, it had been assumed that state education should be the
responsibility of local government authorities — they were 'the market
stallholders'. As a result, large, and in some cases monolithic, bureaucracies

grew up. Local education authorities wielded considerable power and influence through the appointment and allocation of staff, the allocation of budgets, the influence and control of local inspectors and the patronage of education officers.

Many LEAs did an excellent job but the nature and style of an LEA was a significant factor in determining the quality and values of its schools — in determining in fact what was available in the state-education market place. Since the education debate had concluded that schools were failing, it was inevitable that the finger should, to some extent, be pointed at the local authorities.

The 1980s were the age of market forces and value for money. The customer, in the guise of both the parent and the pupil, was apparently being failed. LEAs were regarded as too distant and resistant to market forces — each LEA had a monopoly within its own area. In a period of public-expenditure restraint, their central bureaucracies were also judged expensive. Coupled to all this was the fact that the dominant political ideology in some local authorities was at odds with that of the government in Westminster, and these local authorities in particular, but all LEAs to some extent, were regarded as encouraging egalitarianism in schools at the expense of academic excellence. Parents, it was judged, should have a greater choice presented to them.

As a result, means were found of releasing schools from the shackles of LEAs and of giving the 'customers' more direct influence in the market place by giving them the right of choice. At the same time curbs on LEA central costs were intended to release cash into the schools. The buzz words were powerful and they were 'decentralization', 'delegation', 'devolved responsibility' and 'autonomy'.

The advent of LMS in 1988 was a shock to much of the educational establishment. Far-sighted LEAs had for some years been experimenting with delegated budgets, more had not. Those which had experimented had kept the balance of control at LEA level and the experiments had been on their terms and at their speed. Suddenly the reins were taken out of their hands and the horse was being driven by central government.

Many LEAs were thrown into confusion by the requirement to delegate such large percentages of budget to individual schools and this was made even more unpalatable by the consequent devolvement of responsibility and control to heads and governing bodies. LMS has made it increasingly difficult for LEAs to manage and manipulate funding to achieve LEA objectives. LMS formulae and Section 42 Statements prised open the closed doors of local-authority decision-making and put target setting and resource decisions at school level. Those schools wanted to be confident that they were receiving their fair share of education budgets. Open management, as practised by the few best local authorities, had been forced on all of them.

As local management progressed, LEAs found themselves selling their services to their own schools. The schools had become the customers of the LEAs and the LEAs had to respond to new market forces. Increasingly, the schools were in charge of their own market stalls and independent of their original parent companies. It cannot, however, be denied that many schools were unprepared to have greatness thrust upon them. Suddenly, from managing relatively small books and equipment budgets, governors and senior staff found themselves in charge of budgets of one or more millions. Some heads resisted the impact they saw this would have on their traditional roles as headteachers while others lacked the management competences to cope. Major changes in the management of schools had to take place. These changes would affect not only the way schools were run but also the relationship between school and LEA. The quality of the school's response to this need for change would affect its ability to hold its own in the market place.

Of course, it is now a matter of record that most schools have coped fairly well with their new responsibility but the extent of the structural and cultural changes which LMS has wrought in schools has yet to be comprehensively evaluated. The change is still in the early stages in so many schools and authorities. What can be observed within the schools is that many heads and governing bodies are more management-oriented, possess higher-order management skills and are patently enjoying the new scenario. There has been a radical transformation in the way schools see themselves and others. Many are becoming increasingly confident and, at the same time, analytical and more critical in their evaluation of the roles of other players on the educational stage. The stallholders have changed and the schools have become more important in the market place than the LEAs.

The balance of power has definitely shifted; the status quo has disappeared. I believe there is no more exciting place to be at this time than in a school. It is in schools that the potential and challenges of self-determination are to be realized and it is through seizing the grant maintained initiative that schools will become even more exciting places for all with an interest in the future of education. The record of what happened and is happening in my own school reflects the nature and extent of the changes facing schools during this reforming period and provides evidence of how schools are responding to the challenges presented.

Some schools, like my own, were a little ahead of the game. We had been fortunate in being a pilot school in Cambridgeshire's local financial-management scheme which had begun in 1982. Thus, by 1988 and The Education Reform Act, we had already sniffed the scent of self-determination for six years. We welcomed the national directive and, unlike some schools, we were already committed to the objectives of local management and needed no persuasion of the benefits of devolved responsibility. The 1988 Act confirmed for us our role in the 'market place' and our responsibility to our 'customers'. Gradually, even as early as 1988, as a school we were becoming aware that our increased control of resources was changing fundamentally our relationship with our LEA. The wider interpretation of local management as set out in the 1988 Act contained elements which would challenge that relationship even further and to the point where the option of grant maintained status would become a live issue.

In view of some publicly and privately expressed views on the part of government ministers about the influence of some LEAs on schools, it does not take much to conclude that the 1988 Education Act was intended to present a nationwide challenge to the relationship between schools and local authorities. In fact, it was to challenge the very role and purpose of LEAs and this was to be one of the essential triggers of change, one of the cornerstones of the strategy for improving quality in education, a means of raising standards. Once schools had learned to manage themselves, unless they found a satisfactory answer to 'Why LEAs?', they would ditch the old ties and sail for Byzantium — GMS.

That, almost inevitably I believe, is what happened to the school of which I am head. We did not aim for grant maintained status as a respite from a difficult LEA, nor did we run from a reorganization or the threat of closure. We considered ourselves a successful school and, in 1993, when we took the grant maintained option we had experienced eleven years of increasing self-management which had bred in us a new kind of self-confidence and awareness. We had gone through a learning and maturing experience and, like a post-pubescent child, we were intent on gaining our independence.

Empowering the Customer

It would be ridiculous to see parental choice as a new concept. Some parents had always been able to exercise choice over the school to which they sent their children. However, in 1988, two things changed; parental rights to make such choices were enshrined in legislation and schools were to be funded on the results of that choice — on pupil numbers. This was to create a direct link between the market place and the school. Even more directly, some schools especially where rolls were falling would see a direct link between customer preference and teacher jobs — always a sensitive issue for the profession. There was a need for schools to start paying attention to what the customer wanted.

With the increased requirement for schools to publish information, with the development of league tables, and with decisions such as class size and school recruitment now placed very firmly with the individual school, the LEA has very little influence on or over how parents choose. In fact, as far as most parents active in the search for the school of their choice are concerned, the LEA has become an irrelevance. The question for each school must be to what extent the LEA has a role and how much energy and percentage of its budget the school can divert to being a part of that particular club. Each school must arrive at its own answers. In 1993, with an irrevocably changing relationship between the school and the LEA, and with an increasing awareness that a discerning and empowered customer group regarded us as accountable to them in our own right, our school took the quantum leap into GMS.

The First Challenge of GMS

It is simplistic but not untrue to note that the process of becoming grant maintained has similarities with the risks of floating a company on the stock market. The initial 'flotation' depends, to a large degree on its reputation and ability to create 'shareholder' confidence in the company and its future. The survival of the company after that is dependent on keeping its shareholders and customers happy. The parent ballot is, undoubtedly, the first challenge for the prospective grant maintained school. Choosing the optimum timing and manner for presenting the case to those who will vote is part of that challenge.

Our school's first brush with the idea of GMS came in 1990. The issue had been raised by a parent governor and discussed at governors' meetings during the summer and autumn of that year. To the majority of those who were party to those early discussions, the question was really, 'Why not?' rather than, 'Why?' We had little fear of independence and saw it as the logical step forward in management terms from the experience of LMS. We could, therefore, see all the reasons for taking the grant maintained option but we needed to examine the arguments against.

One of the strongest arguments for us at the time was a local one. Our LEA was developing a vision of locally managed schools operating with all the financial benefits of GMS but within a cooperative network nominally called the LEA. This was a beguiling idea and we were encouraged by officers to stay in the LEA and play our part in developing that vision. Looking back now it is possible to see that there may have been a wish on all our parts not to disturb an established order within which the school had functioned and been successful for the whole of its history. Had we taken the grant maintained step at that time we would have been the first secondary school in our county to do so — we would have been the first breach in the wall.

At another level, there was an awareness in many of our minds of the political uncertainties of GMS. John Major had just been elected to the leadership of the Conservative Party and the media were confidently predicting an election early in 1991. In some of our minds there was a concern that we might hold a ballot and then find a new government in power which threatened to be hostile to the grant maintained idea. We recognized that even a successful ballot would arouse a degree of opposition, leaving some discord behind. We would need to continue to prove that GMS was a good choice for the school for some time into the future — a difficult task in a hostile national political climate. We could even find ourselves unceremoniously relocated into an LEA we had appeared to reject — not a happy prospect.

In December 1990, only three governors were opposed to GMS in principle but the remainder agreed to give the LEA more time to develop its new vision. It was decided to review the matter in a year's time. When the governing body eventually revisited the issue in May 1992, it did so at the same time as a large group of schools in our LEA, and nationally, which had concluded that the grant maintained bandwagon looked, after the 1992 General Election result, as if it would become unstoppable and would outpace the rate of change in any LEA.

When the first and second resolutions to hold a parent ballot were passed by the governing body in the summer of 1992, there was little opposition within the governing body itself. GMS was regarded by most as the natural and obvious next step, the culmination of ten years of increasing self-management and the best way to secure the successful future of the school. The governing body of our school saw its responsibility as to assess the national and local environment and decide the appropriate strategic direction for the school in the long and short terms. Its choice was GMS.

The task in front of us was to convince our parents of the rightness of our conviction. We tried to think these things through in advance but, as ever, when dealing with the public, we were both right and very wrong. During the weeks leading up to, and the weeks spanning, the ballot itself, we were both delighted and shocked by the course of events. Indeed, when asked what I would consider the most difficult and stressful period during my seven years of headship, I never hesitate in identifying the three weeks of the parent ballot for grant maintained status. Events since then have, of course, also made them one of the most rewarding.

The Parents Choose

If grant maintained status is one means of providing diversity within state education, then to be viable the grant maintained option needs to be popular with a significant number of parents. It is essential for the customer to understand how the educational 'product' offered by a grant maintained school differs. In our experience it was also essential, particularly at the time when parents are balloted, for them to understand how it is not different. For every school, marketing is an increasingly important activity but for the grant maintained school there is an additional dimension of which to be aware. A great deal of misinformation about GMS is presented by all kinds of sources. Some of it arises from misunderstanding and some of it from deliberate and partisan presentation of facts by both those against and, at times, those in favour of grant maintained status.

We found that, during the balloting process, our parents had particular questions which could be summarized in the following way:

- Would the school become selective?
- Would the school continue to have the same relationship with its community?
- Would GMS mean a loss of democratic control over the school?
- Would we continue to attract quality teachers to the school?
- Would the school be guilty of depriving other schools of funding?

- What would we lose by removing the school from LEA control?
- Were parents being given full and balanced information?

Some of these concerns, as it can be seen, were about the nature of GMS while others were about the practice. That our vote came out two to one in favour of the school applying for grant maintained status indicates that, on balance, more parents were satisfied on these points than were not. However, before the ballot result there was some fierce debate which at times seemed to veer off the expected path.

It was, nevertheless, essential that all concerned knew where our school stood on each of the issues which concerned them. There is, of course no requirement that a grant maintained school should become selective in any way. However so much has been made in the press of the fact that a grant maintained school has this option, there is a belief in some people's minds that this is an automatic course of action for every grant maintained school. The truth is that any grant maintained school has the right to apply to the Secretary of State for a change in the character of the school but this is not an option of which many schools will want to take advantage and, if they did, the term 'a change of character' could as easily refer to an increase in pupil numbers as becoming selective.

Similarly, there were misconceptions about the make up of the governing body, both as it existed before and as it would exist after incorporation. The focus of this issue was whether parents would have a voice and whether the new status took the school further away from local democracy. This is the subject of a much longer debate than there is room for here. Briefly, a grant maintained governing body has more parent governors than a LEA school because, in addition to its five elected parents, two of its first or foundation governors have to be parents.

However, it is arguable that the grant maintained governing body is less democratically appointed in that, whereas the LEA previously appointed six of the governors, all the non-elected grant maintained governors are appointed by the governing body itself. I say *arguably* because it does depend on how democratic in a local sense the LEA is seen to be in the practice of appointing governors. At least, in the grant maintained governing body, all governors including those elected by teachers and parents have a say in the appointment of other governors.

It was important to our governing body that our parents understood the values that it held and that *comprehensive* and *community* education were first among those. Thus it was that the governing body defined and published a statement of its values which it sent to all parents. This was the first time the governors had ever tried to agree or set out such a statement and it was impressive that there was no fundamental disagreement on any point. It was, in the terms of the market place, a form of mission statement. However, whatever the various issues raised before and during ballot, all of us realized that the outcome rested very largely on the past. It was the reputation and previous performance of the school which either gave, or did not give, parents confidence in the school and in its management. For our school, this appeared to be a major factor in the minds of parents.

As a governing body we learned quickly that the opposition would not only be about the issues — the argument we had expected and had felt fairly confident could be won. It was to be more complex and more invidious. A group of governors met frequently during the pre- ballot and ballot phases in order to respond to events and decide what publicity should go out. They attempted to counteract any misinformation which might be circulating and these governors concluded that, given there was such a large majority in the governing body in favour, it was right for the governors to continue to give a clear lead to parents. Many felt that was their responsibility since they were so much closer to the issues and the practicalities than most parents. The consensus view of those governors was that it was a question of keeping steadfastly to an honest and unambiguous presentation of the case as we saw it. Inevitably it would seem there were those who would interpret this lack of ambiguity as bias. It was this accusation about imbalance in the governors' presentation of information which dogged the argument throughout. This we were to discover was also the experience of several other schools. The opposition rallied to this argument with fervour as it gave grounds for suggesting that parents were not being treated fairly and that this was a poor omen for trusting in the governors if the school were to become grant maintained.

There has been a great deal of debate about the stance it is wise for the head to adopt during a grant maintained ballot and there is, of course, a real difficulty for heads in knowing whether to declare an opinion or to attempt to remain neutral. I chose, after considerable reflection, to declare my hand. At the first meeting held with parents to discuss grant maintained status, there was a relatively large turnout. When it came to my turn to speak I was so convinced that GMS was the best option for the college that I knew I had to be honest and say so. In the longer term that has proved the right choice but, in the heat and politics of the campaign, there were moments when it was not a comfortable option.

Professionally, in the heat of the controversy, I felt very vulnerable. I had declared a commitment to the idea of GMS and, if parents rejected that view, then I felt I should resign from the headship. I began to view the parent ballot partly as a vote of confidence. If the vote went against GMS the parents would be saying they thought I was wrong and I felt that would affect their confidence in my judgment in future. Perversely, I did not regard a yes vote as a declaration of confidence in me personally but an assurance that the parents and I wanted the same future for the school. My conclusion was that a no vote would mean I was the wrong person to continue to lead the school. The outcome became of much greater personal import to me than to other governors.

It was, as might be imagined, an enormous relief when the ballot result was declared. There was a two-thirds majority in favour. Many of us realized afterwards what others had been aware of all the way through, that a great deal of debate had been initiated by only a comparatively few opponents and that some of that may indeed have been politically inspired. However, we had survived the first challenge and our parents had made their decision — Comberton was to become a grant maintained school.

The Wider Implications

From the beginning of the route to GMS, there were those who continually raised the question of how far grant maintained schools would have an adverse effect on the well-being of the system as a whole. Their concerns centred on the effect of diminishing the LEA and its ability to support other schools. It was argued that GMS might benefit the individual school because it would be advantageously funded but this would be to the detriment of schools left in the LEA. It was no good retaliating that all schools had the opportunity to opt out because there was and is a strong belief in many quarters that some schools are so disadvantaged that they could not survive without LEA support. We were accused of seeking our own advantage at the expense of those with greater needs — not a pleasant accusation to try and refute.

There are, of course two points to be answered. The first is that grant maintained schools take more than their fair share out of the system. The second is that LEAs must survive because GMS is not appropriate, and never will be, for some schools. Both points lead to the argument that if the LEA must survive for the sake of weaker schools no school should opt out of the LEA because that threatens the survival of the LEA and, therefore, the survival of those schools which depend on it. The argument is, I believe, not sustainable.

Some early grant maintained schools, it must be admitted, were favourably funded. They took a share out of the LEA central budget equivalent to 15 per cent of the school's delegated budget. This add-on or central element did bite into the central budgets particularly of LEAs which were delegating more than the percentage norm to schools through LMS budgets. Occasionally this created a situation where a grant maintained school could be receiving more than 100 per cent of its fair budget share.

Since 1993 this has changed and the add-on for any school incorporated on or after 1 April 1993 is calculated on the actual percentage of central budget which is appropriate for its individual LEA. The grant maintained school, therefore, gets no more and no less than its fair share and this is effectively the same as the amount which the LEA retains centrally for each of its schools. This is the money normally used by LEAs to provide central services and administration for its schools. It stands to reason that, if a school is no longer provided for by its LEA, and grant maintained schools are not, that money needs to be in the school itself so it can provide for itself.

Some opponents point to the extra grants which grant maintained schools can bid for as evidence that the sector is creaming off money which should be put into schools generally. The argument may be emotive but it is not founded on fact. LEAs bid for numerous education grants from central government. Some of these include training and development funds and money for capital projects. Grant maintained schools can do the same, the only difference being that they do so individually. The levels of these grants and the criteria for granting them appear very similar. The only additional money that a grant maintained school collects is its transitional grant to enable it to set up as a self-governing school.

Despite all these facts to the contrary, LEAs still shout foul and produce statistics to show the reductions in overall budget which they blame on grant maintained schools. Less is usually said about the savings that are or should be possible because that LEA has fewer schools to support. I was recently rung by the local paper because an LEA had produced a press release to draw attention to the fact that its maintenance budget had been reduced by central government. It was laying the blame at the door of the GMS sector and particularly the schools in its county which had become grant maintained. It had not stated that there may have been a reduction in provision because it was no longer required to maintain over a third of its erstwhile secondary schools because they had become grant maintained.

LEAs and their supporters are convinced that, even if the deductions from LEA revenue could be shown to be pro rata, there is still an argument that the net effect is to decimate central services to the point where it is not possible to employ staff and to maintain expertise in order to provide for remaining schools. The strength of the LEA, it is maintained, arises from the fact that the sum of its parts together is greater than the sum of its parts separately.

There does appear to be a contradiction in the reasoning at this point. If a grant maintained school is able to provide for itself on the funds that it receives, and if, as I have argued, these funds are only equal to the school's fair share, how can it be that the LEA cannot do so for its schools collectively on what is left. Perhaps the answer lies in the costly structures which a local authority must support in addition to its direct services.

On then to the argument that LEAs are essential because there will always be schools which need that kind of support. The corollary is to maintain that some schools could never survive as grant maintained. It is often assumed that in this category come many small primary schools and those schools which serve pupils with social or learning disadvantages. Those who befriend this argument do seem unable to let go of their historical blinkers. They appear to overlook the realities of LMS which, in any event, prevent an LEA pouring funding into any school in order to provide individual support for needy schools. Indeed all the funding which LEA schools receive is determined by the formula budget and the same formula is also used for determining the annual maintenance grant for grant maintained schools. Those schools where there is a high level of pupils needing support receive the same level of support under LMS or GMS rules. Nor is the argument about small schools as strong as it appears. It is perfectly possible for grant maintained schools to share costs by grouping together to provide or purchase what they may need. Indeed, I believe that this is a significant recent development amongst groups of large and small grant maintained schools and one my school has been happy to cooperate with.

A number of grant maintained schools locally has in the last year grouped together to buy consultant time to undertake work which everyone needed done. One of these projects was to negotiate a contract for community education between the grant maintained schools and the local authority and another was to take up with the Department for Education the case for higher percentage central AMGs. This kind of work is comparable to that done by LEA Officers for LEA schools but in these instances it has been bought and paid for at a fraction of the cost to each school. There is scope for increasing this kind of cooperation and this is happening in our own area and elsewhere.

I am, therefore, inclined to the view that very few schools, if any, would not be able to survive outside of an LEA if they wished to do so. If they do not wish to take that course it is their decision but that cannot be an acceptable argument for preventing others from opting out. I would go even further and challenge those that choose to remain in LEAs to examine carefully what evidence they believe they have that what has always been is always going to be the best choice. Indeed there are times when what has been appropriate assumes some of the properties of a white elephant.

Making GMS Work

At the time of writing, our school has been grant maintained for nearly a year — time to have taken stock of the position we are now in and the realities of self-government and undoubtedly like most grant maintained schools we feel we have something to prove. We are determined to get it right and to justify our parents confidence in us. In order to do that we have to be alert to the potential but also to the pitfalls lurking in the undergrowth.

One of these pitfalls is the possibility of almost unconsciously recreating the disadvantages of an LEA. We could find ourselves spending more and more on in-house support structures because our background of LEA support is a strong influence and may still be a curb on our self-reliance. For example, as a school, we could buy in enormous amounts of backup — information technology, boiler-maintenance plans, property management, personnel advice, library support, health and safety advice etc.

Much of this could be seen as essential or wise purchases. However, the cost can be a creeping paralysis and there are many providers of services luring us to buy their wares. In this respect the battle for the grant maintained school is not so different from that of the LEA — it is the need to control central overheads in order to direct resources to teaching and learning. For the individual school this can be significantly easier than for an authority because it is easier to avoid large bureaucratic structures and also easier to analyse costs on a unit-cost basis. Being so much closer to the pupils and their parents keeps the real needs very prominently in mind.

This closeness to parents is true for all schools but our first year's experience would suggest that there is a deeper bond between us and our 'customers' because there is no LEA acting as third party. This has been good. In a very small way it was illustrated by the admissions process. This year we received a record number of requests for admission. We cooperated with the LEA very successfully in coordinating admissions processes because we felt there were benefits all round — for us, for parents and pupils, for the LEA. However, we were able to make our own decisions on numbers of admissions and this was based on the realities and practicalities of our school as well as the future needs of the area and of the school. No one was turned down. Indeed, the fact that we sent out our own letters offering places and were able to personalize those letters and include a whole host of relevant and reassuring information for parents and pupils has been much appreciated. Our relationships with new parents and pupils has been enhanced at the outset.

It is of course in the area of planning that we shall have to see how the relationship of the school, LEA and Funding Agency works out. There are two important aspects: the planning authorities as a whole need to be sure that sufficient school places are provided in an area, the school needs to be able to determine its own future and have access to essential data. There is no reason why, in future, it should not be possible to approach such matters in a spirit of partnership.

During this first year of grant maintained status we have had an interesting and apparently unique experience as a grant maintained school. A planning decision for a new settlement in our area has produced a requirement for a significant additional number of places in our school. We have worked with the County Council and the District Council but we have also negotiated very successfully ourselves with the developer for a major contribution to the cost of expanding the school. There are obviously risks and uncertainties about any such plans but certainly we feel a great deal closer to the process and more in control of the outcomes than we might have done as an LEA school. We are truly partners in the planning process. This experience, of course, predates the advent of the Funding Agency for Schools and it remains to be seen how that body will operate in relationship to the existing planning authorities. However, for grant maintained schools, it must be a reassurance that this body will be able to oversee the interests of the GMS sector since the LEA may well have particular interest in its own schools.

There are of course many factors which may influence matters in the near future. The impending change to unitary authorities makes it probable that existing local authorities will be superseded. This prospect worries many LEA schools because they fear that there is likely to be a lack of educational expertise around in the new authorities. The break-up of LEAs also undermines the arguments about protection of weaker schools. LEAs of the future are likely to be smaller and less protective. Certainly, it should be expected that local-authority reorganization will provoke serious consideration of the grant maintained option in many governing bodies.

As ever in the public sector, levels and means of funding are crucial issues. Current plans to trial a common funding formula in some LEAs are promising in that it starts to look at ways of equalizing the unequal. However, there are many of us who would prefer the funding itself to be common and not just the formula of distribution. Until there is some equality in local-authority standard-spending assessments that possibility seems very remote.

A constant thorn in the side of the average grant maintained school is the power of its old LEA to determine the grant maintained school's annual maintenance grant through the setting of its schools' budget and the determining of the funding formula. A great deal of the time of many GMS heads is spent on scrutinizing Section 42 statements and writing letters to central and local government on the various machinations of those who locally determine funding and who sometimes appear to do so with understandable bias against schools who have opted out of their control. Few in the grant maintained sector can be unhappy about the advent of the concept of some common basis of funding distribution which leaves less room for local politics to affect the spending on pupils' education.

No Turning Back

There can be no turning back for schools which have set their faces to a GMS future, nor do I know of any which could face the prospect with equanimity. It is a journey which, for us, started with increased financial responsibility and which led to independence but which has yet more potential to lead us further along a road, the destination of which we can only glimpse. Once started, the journey must continue: none can realistically envisage a grant maintained school fitting happily back into its former LEA and, if the grant maintained option has proved popular with parents, it will be a brave Secretary of State who tries to reverse the legislation.

There are particular characteristics of the grant maintained school and they are:

- independence;
- responsibility;
- accountability; and
- and the motivation to get it right.

The increased responsibility of governors and staff makes it impossible to pass the buck far. Accountability is to the parents and children, not through any third party but directly from school to home. This increases the importance of that relationship and improves its clarity. The grant maintained school can provide an attractive option for the 'customer' because it has the ability to develop its own ethos and character and to respond in a new way to the needs of its pupils. Much of this potential has yet to be realized and it will become more apparent as the GMS sector grows and we stop fighting yesterday's battles over power and control and grasp fully the possibilities we have unleashed.

In ten years time it is possible that LEAs will have become unrecognizable as their present selves and that all schools will be operating in some form of independent state. Whatever happens, I believe the grant maintained option will have changed the way that education is organized in England and Wales for all time and for the better.

Chapter 6

Managing the Market

Peter Downes

Some Doubts about the Market Place Philosophy

I suspect that the majority of headteachers do not feel comfortable with the concept of the market place in the school sector. All of those who are now holding senior positions in schools started their careers at a time when teachers felt themselves to be part of a public service dedicated to improving education for all children in the country. True, your immediate commitment was to the school in which you were teaching and in particular to those pupils in your classes. 'Pride in the school' was a theme frequently mentioned at assemblies and prize days but it was predominantly aimed at raising the level of behaviour and performance of the individuals in the school (and reducing the time spent by heads on fielding complaints from local residents) rather than enabling the school to compete against other schools, other than in the specific area of sports fixtures.

The combination of measures taken by the government over the last ten years has radically changed the climate in schools. The 1988 Education Act, leading to local management of schools (LMS), greater parental choice, the creation of grant maintained schools, the centralization of the curriculum and the publication of league tables of academic results and truancy have all been based on the idea that competition raises standards. Such is the complexity of the educational process, it is unclear whether or not that hypothesis can ever be soundly tested. For example, it is now quite clear that academic standards, as measured by examination results at 16 and 18, rose during the 1980s but *before* the full effect of the market philosophy had been felt. If standards continue to rise, will it be because of what the government has done or would they have risen anyway?

The central moral objection to the market place ethos in the compulsory educational sector is that in the real market place, there are *losers* as well as winners. The local traders who sell shoddy goods, look dirty and disorganized, are grumpy to customers and do nothing to make their products known to the public, go out of business. They are the ones to suffer directly from their own incompetence and mismanagement; indirectly, their immediate families may well suffer hardship; the goods they are selling, being inanimate, are not penalized by their misfortune in being displayed on their shelves. An under-performing school harms its own products. Under the LMS system, which links income very closely to the number of pupils on roll (an ostensibly sensible idea), a dwindling school finds itself in an increasingly difficult position as its fixed costs remain virtually stable and it suffers from a diseconomy of scale (Knight, 1993). The serious weakness in the market philosophy applied to schools is that schools do not fail and close down rapidly. They may take years to become totally unviable and during those years several hundred children may have been receiving a substandard education which is *the only one* they are going to get.

The opponents of the market-led and consumerist approach argue that those responsible for a national education system should be aiming to raise achievement *for all*, should be projecting a vision of society as involving interdependent relationships and should be seeing education as the transmission of human culture rather than as a production-line for entrepreneurs (Wragg, 1993). Some go further and consider that the entire movement towards self-managing schools is a 'cruel hoax', nothing more than 'the privatization of education based on a culture of competitive and possessive individualism' (Smith, 1993). They see the whole process as having been driven by a political rather than an educational agenda, a 'centralism which strikes at the heart of democracy'.

Coming to Terms with the Market Place

Some heads (including Rosalie Clayton who also contributes to this volume) take a more positive view of the market place in education and even those who share the reservations expressed above come to terms with their worries by trying to look for ways in which they can turn evil into good. They argue that 'marketing' should not be considered as 'trying to persuade reluctant purchasers to buy a product' but should be considered rather as being 'increasingly sensitive to the needs of the customers'. In this way they reconcile their innate 'public service philosophy' with the new expectations of the educational scene. There is some debate about who exactly the 'customers' are. Is it the parents or the pupils? Technically it is the parents who choose the secondary school but surveys have suggested that the pupils' preference is highly influential. Defining parents as 'customers' raises problems: the good school may prefer to see parents as partners in the educational process rather than as consumers of a product. Once the pupils are in the school, their needs are paramount and they become the 'customers'. Clearly the parents continue to exercise considerable influence and have the legal responsibility for their children's education. For most of the time, the wishes of pupils and parents overlap but there may be occasions when the school has to intercede when there are differences of opinion e.g., when options are being chosen or post-16 courses are being considered.

Taking the market place view means recognizing that the days when schools had set packages and immutable practices to offer to pupils have gone. A good school listens to what pupils and parents want and seeks to inform and involve them as much as possible. In practical terms this means:

- keeping parents fully informed about *general* developments in the curriculum, by means of regular articles in a parents' association news-letter, by open meetings to which parents are invited to meet heads of department who explain what is happening in their particular subject and by full briefings (meetings and documentation) when parents and pupils have to make significant decisions about course choices and options;
- making sure that parents are fully informed about the progress of their own *individual* children, by regular reports, parents' evenings, interim work/effort assessments and by a policy of early contact with parents by pastoral staff when there are any concerns;
- involving parents in the national debates on educational trends, by encouraging parents' associations to regard educational issues as being of equal importance to the traditional social and fund-raising aspects of their activities;
- making parents realize that the school is ready to listen to their worries and that we regard their input to the education of their children as being of crucial importance;
- involving pupils in their own progress as individuals by encouraging them to discuss their academic development with teachers and tutors in a relaxed, open and trusting way and by valuing the ideas they may have about ways in which they could learn more effectively; and
- involving pupils collectively by structuring a system of elected councils to enable the pupil voice to be genuinely heard on a range of issues which are within their competence, given that schools are not yet run on totally democratic lines and that teachers and heads have to make the final decisions.

A consistent policy of openness to customer reaction along these lines can build up confidence and trust. Those of us who have spent most of our lives in the school setting easily forget that many parents are 'detached' from their children's schooling (particularly in the secondary sector where the subject content gets harder). Indeed, some are alienated from schools as establishments because of their own unhappy experience of it. We are only just seeing the first cohorts of secondary-age pupils who are the children of parents who were not themselves stigmatized by failure at 11+. We therefore need to work very hard at explaining to parents the school's aims and objectives, its values and its methods; we need to explain educational jargon and the unending proliferation of acronyms. In this way we can build up parental confidence in the school, its staff and what it offers and this interpretation of 'marketing' is wholly positive. (See Beischer 1993 for a constructive illustration.)

It is the parents of pupils currently and recently in the school who are the most potent force for 'selling' the school to other parents. There are other direct methods of 'promoting' the school which we will look at later but none is as powerful as the word-of-mouth recommendation of a satisfied customer. The casual word over the garden fence, in the bus queue or in the supermarket means far more than dozens of glossy brochures or the more blatant promotion techniques which are being adopted.

Presenting the School in the Best Light

Notwithstanding the primary importance of good customer/pupil/parent relations, schools are becoming increasingly conscious of the importance of presenting themselves positively. There is nothing wrong in this in itself provided that the product and the promotional message match up. The Trades Description laws may not yet have been applied to educational marketing but that does not mean that heads should fail to check the truth of the projected image. There is a tension between the imperative of survival in the market place and the absolute commitment to 'truth'. This tension can be resolved in a number of ways, depending on whether the medium of communication is oral or written. A school prospectus should not make false claims, e.g., team games against other schools are played every Saturday morning, when that is clearly not the case. Skilful writers of prospectuses draw attention to the good features of the school while failing to mention those negatives which might deter prospective customers. The head is more personally exposed when taking questions at the open evenings for potential new parents which take place in October and November. A direct question about the examination statistics has to be answered honestly. If the English results at GCSE are clearly not very good, it is better, in my view, for the head to recognize this and go on to say what is being done about it than to pretend that there is not a problem. Parents are now asking about the school's approach to matters on the social/ educational border (drugs, smoking, sex). The head who pretends that there are no problems is unlikely to be persuasive, simply because the questioner will already know that there are difficulties. Better by far to show an awareness of the issues and talk about an action plan to deal with them rather then to pretend they do not exist.

Even without straying into these controversial areas, there is much that can be done to smarten up the image. Heads are increasingly paying more attention, for example, to ensuring that

- the school notepaper has a modern style and that all publications produced by the school are well designed, accurate, free from spelling mistakes and written at a level which is comprehensible to parents (including versions in minority languages where that is relevant);
- the school site is signposted in such a way that the hesitant visitor can easily find the way to the place or person they need to contact;
- displayed material in public areas (foyers, corridors and halls) is up-to-date, attractive and colourful. Primary schools have an excellent record in displaying pupils' work and secondary schools are gradually catching up, with photographic records of pupils' activities and achievements, posters for events, exhibits of pupils' art and sculpture work, information about the school's charity work, overseas links — all helping to convey to visitors that they are in contact with a school which is alive and has confidence in what it is aiming to achieve. A positive by-product of an up-beat policy on display is that, as well as appealing to the visitor, it can raise morale among the staff and pupils currently working in the school.
- every occasion when parents come into school (parents' evenings, concerts, plays, PTA events) is fully exploited by having high-profile presence by the senior staff, clear notices of welcome and relevant information, advertisements for forthcoming events, sale of school magazines, coffee and refreshments; in other words no trouble is spared in making sure that the visit of a parent into the school is a warm, friendly and successful experience.

Marketing Outside the School

While it is clearly important to project a good image of the school to those who set foot inside it, it is just as important to make sure that the school is well thought of in the local community. Many secondary schools are now taking a more positive approach to liaison with primary schools, principally in order to improve the continuity of learning from Keystage 2 to 3 but also to make sure that, in those areas where parents do have a genuine range of alternatives at secondary-transfer point, the parents of primary children are made aware of the distinctive features of the secondary school. In addition to the professional liaison in curriculum matters, more and more secondary schools are giving primary pupils 'taster-days', or are setting up joint projects where primary and lower-secondary pupils are working together. In other cases secondary-school teachers work with primary colleagues in specialist areas, or invite primary pupils into secondary schools to work in laboratories, or to play with the secondary school orchestra. Some secondary schools organize sports tournaments for local primary schools which bring parents into the secondary school grounds in a context which creates positive feelings. All these activities are worthwhile in themselves and it would be cynical to regard them merely as marketing ploys but there is no doubt that they do help to generate positive attitudes towards particular secondary schools.

The thrust towards marketing within the local community is not confined to primary schools. Many schools work hard at public relations on a number of fronts:

- They develop much closer relations with the local press, often having a designated member of staff as press officer, making sure that the local press has a regular supply of newsworthy stories.
- They take part in local events, festivals, and competitions, involving local commerce, Rotary and Town Twinning Associations, for example.
- They bring local companies into school as frequently as they can to support young enterprise, to give mock job-interviews, to help with careers advice and to sponsor school activities.
- They are increasingly encouraging the local community to use school premises for events (trade fairs, seminars, conferences, weddings, antiques fairs, bring-and-buy sales), not only because such bookings bring revenue into the school but because the more frequently local people can come into the school buildings in a context which gives them pleasure and service, the greater will be the esteem in which the school is held. This only holds true, of course, if the quality of service given is excellent; a grumpy caretaker, failed heating and lukewarm coffee do not do much good to the school's local standing!

The Impact of a Marketing Approach on the Head and Deputies

All the above section shows how more specific marketing is developing in the school sector. The argument which many would put forward is that all these are long-standing examples of good practice which have simply been increased by the market place ethic. There is no doubt that it has had a significant effect on the work of heads and deputies who are expected to take the lead in such developments, for which they will have had little specialized training and in which they may not have the specific skills which are required. Traditionally heads have come to headship from being a successful deputy, having previously been successful as a head of house or department, which post they achieved principally by being good classroom teachers. The demands of headship in the 1990s are much wider than even a decade ago and that it is why

it is increasingly important for those aiming for headship to undergo management training to develop the broader skills which are required. Some would
even argue that people should not be allowed to apply for headship posts
without having a certificate of satisfactory participation in a headship prepara-
tion course of the kind offered by the National Education Assessment Centre
in Oxford.

In schools which are still fairly new to LMS, heads find an increasing
proportion of their time taken up with managerial issues not directly related
to educational content. In some schools which have had longer experience,
much of the marketing detail is left by the head to a bursar so that the head
can concentrate on the academic, curricular and pastoral aspects of the post
which he or she sees as being his or her overriding priority. It must be
recognized that, even where there is an effective bursar in post, the public
expectation is that the head will be the focal point for the public relations
activities of the school. It is not something that the head can shoulder alone,
however. This is where team work with deputies and other senior staff is
essential if the head is going to survive the pressure. The projection to the
parents and to the wider public must be of a senior team whose members,
while having particular management and administrative specialisms, are all
involved in seeing that the school is well marketed, in the best and most
positive sense of the word.

Within the professional circles of heads and deputies, opinion is divided
on whether the market approach corrodes educational leadership. Some have
'gone through the marketing phase' to achieve a sensible balance between the
imperatives of the market and educational leadership; others have become
trapped in the jargon and thinking of the market place.

It is still too soon to tell whether or not the transition from enhanced
LMS (i.e., within an LEA policy of maximum delegation) to GMS (total
autonomy within central government cash constraints) distorts the outlook of
senior managers in schools. Many of the most experienced GMS school heads
went straight to GMS from pre-LMS structures and in a minority of cases this
was because they genuinely wanted to embrace the greater freedom that GMS
offers. It has been noticeable that some GMS heads have become highly entrepreneurial and, having embraced one part of the government's philosophy,
have taken a more positive view of other developments, such as the opportunity to introduce performance-related pay schemes, or to set up as a school-
based provider of initial teacher training.

The increased 'managerialization' of heads and deputies has both positive
and negative effects. In dealing with those outside the school, the head as
super-manager finds him- or herself 'speaking the same language' as many of
the parents and the local community. It is sometimes said that the greater
financial awareness of heads has brought them increased respect among the
local business community. The negative effects can be seen in terms of relations within the school. The bulk of the staff is not predominantly concerned

with the market place. They want to do a good job with their classes day by day and they can rightly resent a head or deputy who appears to walking constantly along the mountain-tops without any awareness of what is happening down in the valley. The challenge for the head of the 1990s and beyond is to reconcile these different expectations: on the one hand, to meet the demands of the market place and on the other to remain responsive to the day-to-day direct educational concerns of teaching colleagues. The most skilful will manage to persuade all staff that enhanced performance in all aspects of the school's life is the most powerful marketing tool the head can use. In other words, the head and deputies are not engaged in an activity which stands in opposition to the educational purpose of the school but are dependent for their success (and the school's viability) on the overall efforts of all.

Managing the Finances of Market 'Success'

Every pupil who joins the school brings with him or her a sum of money, the value of which depends on the age of the pupil, varying from, say, £1,500 for a pupil in Years 7–9 through to £2,500 for a sixth-former. Part of the skill of managing market success is to balance the number of pupils in the school with the cost of educating them effectively. An effective marketing head may increase the school's intake in Year 7 from 145 to 155 and may be tempted to feel proud of the success achieved, until it is realized that the school will need to provide an extra teaching group at an annual cost of £25,000, against which can be set the extra income of £15,000. The school's 'success' has been counter-productive in financial terms and will continue to be so for several years, giving a financial disbenefit of £50,000 over the five-year period to Year 11. The head who wants to optimize income and expenditure has to try to keep within an agreed class size and yet keep the classes as full as possible. If you really want to fine-tune this balance, it is best to have a cohort of six, eight or ten class groups so that classes can be paired for those subjects (design) where teaching groups have to be nearer twenty than thirty. The extra money earned by going up from six to seven forms of entry, especially if it produces small teaching groups e.g., 190 pupils in seven groups, will be further wasted on having uneconomical sets for design. Such detailed consideration did not matter a few years ago when LMS was not in place and teachers were provided by the LEA on a linear pupil–teacher-ratio basis. Even in the early days of LMS, when money seemed relatively plentiful, few heads worried themselves about such niceties but in the straightened circumstances of a country in deep recession and decreasing expenditure (relative to demographic growth) on education, such considerations weigh more heavily. The ideal situation is for a school to be just sufficiently over-subscribed for it to be sure of filling itself to its optimum size each year.

Peter Downes

The Strategic Implications of the Market Philosophy

One of the government's assumptions seems to be that 'good schools' will expand to meet public demand but this has to be challenged. All schools have a capacity, both the official one laid down by the Department for Education's guidelines in terms of square metres per pupil, and the unofficial one which the members of the school community feel more instinctively. Every school needs some breathing space in its buildings, in its circulation areas and in its playground capacity. Overfilling a school with pupils could quickly destroy some of the very qualities which have made it attractive in the first place. Bringing in temporary classrooms is rarely a satisfactory expedient and it takes several years to get a building scheme accepted, designed and completed. Conversely a school with lots of spare places is financially unviable. Rarely can spare classrooms be moth-balled or heating systems adjusted to prevent waste of energy.

It is in this area of strategic planning and making the best use of scarce public resources that the market place philosophy runs into its greatest difficulties. Before the 1988 Act and the 1993 creation of the funding agency for schools (FAS), local education authorities (LEAs) tried to match up places to costs so that schools could run at the most cost-effective level for the benefit of all. Strategic planning in the future seems fraught with difficulties. The LEAs will 'share' with the FAS the responsibility of planning school buildings and closures when between 10 per cent and 75 per cent of pupils are in schools which are grant maintained. It remains to be seen how this joint responsibility will be exercised. The inherent difficulty is that the FAS is a creation of government to oversee what is expected to be a predominantly grant maintained sector. Its in-built assumptions are those of the market place and it will be very difficult for it to be seen to be curbing the expansion of those schools which are achieving success in relation to the government's own criteria (parental demand). The LEA strategic planners have a different agenda: they need to get the best possible value for money from the diminishing grant they are receiving and that means trying to balance school intakes to existing buildings, reducing the need to invest heavily in capital-building programmes so that money can be put into improving the condition of existing buildings which are deteriorating year by year.

To get the best value for money overall, it would be better if all the schools in an LEA area were either entirely grant maintained or entirely LEA-controlled. The mixed economy, inevitable as long as the government insists on parents choosing whether or not 'their' school should go grant maintained, is doomed to be cost-ineffective. Such are the financial complexities of the issues that, at the moment of voting, a parent can scarcely be expected to understand what is best for the school, their own school, let alone grasp the implications for all the other schools in the locality. Opinion is divided on the degree of responsibility a head holds for bringing these issues to the attention of parents. My view would be that a head has a moral obligation to expose to his or her parent body what the financial effects of their decision will be on others, difficult though it is to be precise. Under the present financial arrangements, an opt-out decision brings to a school a larger share of the educational cake. Pro-GMS heads argue that this is fair because they have taken on extra responsibility. Others would argue that the extra share of the cake is greater than the extra responsibility needs to entail and therefore somebody else must be suffering. On the other hand, the head also has the responsibility to point out the effect on the school of not going grant maintained, i.e., it is contributing some of the money it needs to those schools which have voted to opt out. The moral argument is bedevilled by a lack of clarity about the way education is funded in the first place. We do not know for sure how the budget for the national educational service is generated nor do we fully understand how it is distributed. Empirically we know that grant maintained schools have more money with which to deliver their educational service, even after they have had to buy in the services they used to get 'free' from the LEA, than LEA schools, yet we are not totally sure where that money has come from. In my wilder moments, I speculate on what would have happened if, in the weeks after the April 1992 General Election, every school in the country had voted to go grant maintained. Would the government have been able to find the extra money and where would it have come from?

The Unresolved Dilemma

This chapter began with a frank admission of the dilemma that faces heads today i.e. the conflict between membership of the public-service sector as a whole and the commitment to an individual school. Nowhere is this dilemma more sharply focused than in the debate on GMS which takes place in a governing body when deciding on whether to invite parents to ballot, and subsequently in the debate which the parents then have before voting. The issues raised in the preceding paragraph cannot be ducked.

In spite of the current government tendency to be 'economical with the truth' which, in this context, could mean a head not drawing the moral dimension of the market place argument to the attention of parents, I remain of the view that professional integrity requires leaders to be as open as they can in order that every voter can make the decision in the light of knowledge rather than ignorance and prejudice. The skills of promotion, marketing and financial fine-tuning can all be mastered eventually but the nettle of the moral dilemma has to be grasped.

References

BEISCHER, N. (1993) 'Expanding schools', *Managing Schools Today*, 3, 3, pp. 36–39.
FORSTER, P. and IVES, M. (1993) *Practical Ideas for Promoting your School*, Harrogate, School Marketing.

Peter Downes

Knight, B. (1993) *Financial Management for Schools: The Thinking Manager's Guide*, London, Heinemann.
Smyth, J. (1993) *A Socially Critical View of the Self-Managing School*, London, The Falmer Press.
Wragg, E. (1993) *A Different Vision*, London, Institute for Public Policy Research.

Chapter 7

Parents: Customers or Partners?

David Bridges

Introduction

Competing conceptualizations of the relationship between parents and schools reflect different views of, among other things, the roles, rights and responsibilities of parents, the conditions under which schools will work most effectively, the professionalism or otherwise of teachers and the circumstances in which children's learning most effectively takes place. The concern of this chapter is to review something of this range of competing conceptualizations. In particular it will focus on parents as puzzled bystanders; supporters; partners; governors; coeducators and customers. The chapter will discuss the evidence and arguments adduced in support of some of these different roles in the context of changing policy and expectations in education in England and Wales since the publication of the Plowden Report in 1967.

Parents as Puzzled Bystanders

One of the no doubt unintended, but foolishly disregarded, consequences of educational developments in the 1960s and 1970s in England and Wales was an increasing sense of puzzlement and disenfranchisement among parents in relation to the education of their children. It was not that parents had previously had any very intimate or active involvement with schools, but there was a number of developments which combined to reinforce their sense of distance and helplessness — of being puzzled and impotent bystanders to the education which their children were receiving. The Plowden Report, for example, reported in 1967 that while there was little evidence among parents of dissatisfaction with schools, 'about half of the parents said they would have liked to be told more about how their children were getting on at school. Almost a third thought that the teachers should have asked them more about their children.' (Central Advisory Council for Education, 1967)

Teaching itself was becoming less of a craft, intelligible and in a modest way able to be imitated by parents, and more of a profession, rendered increasingly esoteric by the advanced educational standards of its degree-bearing members and its changed and increasingly specialized language. This language was drawn from psychology, sociology and philosophy as well as the developing intra-professional discourse associated with 'progressive' education in primary schools and with the working out in curricular and pedagogic terms of the implications of comprehensive secondary schooling. The curriculum content was changing too in ways which rendered the school-learned knowledge of many parents obsolete. Even those who had been relatively successful in their own days at, for example, mathematics found themselves confounded by the maths their own children were doing even in primary school. Ten years after Plowden, the Taylor Report was still warning that 'modern developments in curriculum theory and practice have puzzled and worried many people not involved in school education (Taylor, 1977).

With hindsight it is easy to see that the schools and the teaching profession, caught up in their own enthusiasm for change, made the political and perhaps even moral mistake of failing to keep parents and the community engaged with the changes taking place, failing to communicate to them effectively, and failing to secure parents' informed support. Worse, in some cases, schools reacted defensively to parents' questioning, particularly when that questioning was presented on the basis not of the deferential ignorance of the humble but the informed scepticism of a growing proportion of parents with educational qualifications equivalent to those of the teachers themselves. In such contexts schools were tempted to protect their practice by keeping parents at a distance and controlling their access to its mysteries.

The picture was of course never as simple as I have described it here, and we need to resist the temptation to construct *post hoc* the mythology necessary to explain, or to provide political legitimation for subsequent developments. The late 1970s rhetoric of 'partnership' and 'parent power' and the later measures concerned with national curriculum and assessment, the publication of league tables, parental choice and the 'parents' charter — all these need the kind of story I have told to justify themselves. But throughout the 1960s and 1970s there were other currents running through schools which presented a different picture of parent–school relations.

Both the landmark and highly influential reports on schooling published in the 1960s — Plowden and Newsom — recognized the importance of the parental contribution to children's development and the impact of home circumstances on school achievement. Newsom quotes headteachers' concerns at the impact of parental neglect on the school performance of some pupils: '. . . as one examines the background of these pupils, descending from the more able to the less able, the more one finds them being left to their own devices . . . parents are often over-generous with material things, and under-generous in giving their time to their children' (Central Advisory Council for Education, 1963). Plowden observed, in similar terms, that: 'A strengthening of parental encouragement may produce better performance in school, and this stimulates the parents to encourage more; or discouragement in the home may initiate a vicious downward circle' (Plowden, 1967).

There was, however, little doubt, at least until the watershed of the William Tyndale affair (see Auld, 1976), about where authority on educational matters lay. If children were failing educationally it was the fault not of the school but of economically and culturally disadvantaged parents (or so went the fashionable analysis). The remedy lay in their social and economic improvement and in their being assisted by schools and others in understanding better how to provide home conditions (encouragement, books, conversation, a place to study quietly) better suited to the educational requirements of the schools. This was parental enablement of a kind, but of a kind which reminded them firmly of their subordinate position in the educational process.

Parents as Supporters

The notion that children's educational failure might be blamed on parents' failure to provide the right kind of home support for their children is, not unnaturally, attractive to schools, who are thus exempted from at least some proportion of the blame for such failure. That parents should support the work of schools in a variety of ways was perhaps even more attractive.

Indeed the kind of social and political changes which took place in the 1970s and 1980s reinforced teachers in a growing realization that they needed parental support on a variety of fronts — in maintaining discipline and order among a school population less and less inhibited by regard for the traditional authority of teachers; in counteracting the mounting stridency of public criticism of schools from politicians and the press; in supplementing less and less generous public funding for schools in a context of decaying facilities and rising expectations for the provision of expensive new equipment like computers and video cameras. Some schools, threatened with closure as a result of shifting populations, falling rolls and the need for local-authority economies came to owe their very survival to parental support. Local politicians quickly came to realize that local council seats could be won or lost on the issue of school closure, such was the voting power of the parental lobby. In a hung council like Cambridgeshire between 1985 and 1989 it became virtually impossible for the LEA to close a school. Any party threatening to close one would be faced by two others competing for the local political credit for keeping it open.

Headteachers often talk with satisfaction and comfort about having 'supportive parents' or with frustration about the absence of such support. But what more precisely are the ingredients of such support? I suggest that there are six.

- Parents ensure, as far as this is within their domain, that pupils act in accordance with school requirements e.g., with respect to dress, attendance, homework.

- Parents support the school in maintaining its code of behaviour and more particularly in the event that it needs to take action to enforce that code on a reluctant or 'disruptive' child.
- Parents support school events e.g., concerts, sports days, parents' evenings.
- Parents contribute to school fund-raising activity either directly (e.g., to the school fund) or indirectly through help at a rummage sale or the sale of raffle tickets. Increasingly perhaps schools look to parents as the means of access to local companies which may give sponsorship, professional advice or discounted goods on a significantly greater scale than the school is likely to receive from individuals.
- Parents play an active part as e.g., members of a PTA or as parent governors.
- Parents play a more overtly political role in defending the school or the school's interests in the local community, acting perhaps as a pressure group on the local council or the local MP.

The expectation that schools should receive the unreserved support of parents in the kind of terms set out here cannot pass, and of course has not passed, without question. In what circumstances should parents feel an obligation, for example, to support a code of dress or behaviour or forms of disciplinary action espoused by the school? Is such an obligation owed automatically to a school? Should parents who are opposed in principle to, say, competitive sports or to a school's choice of a play which they hold to be offensive nevertheless feel an obligation to support these events?

In the normal way of things one would surely expect any such obligation to be affected by, for example: whether or not the parents had any choice in the matter of which school their child should attend; whether or not the values implicit in the school codes are compatible with those of the parents; whether or not parents were given the opportunity to contribute through some reasonable process of consultation or decision-making to the code of conduct which they are now invited to support. If parents have no choice and no part in the matter, then it is difficult to see how they could be held to feel any *moral* obligation to support the school, though they might choose to do so prudentially, out of sheer expediency, reckoning that it was in general in the best interests of their child to do so. If parents have a reasonable choice of schools representing a variety of social values and codes including ones to which they were basically sympathetic, then it could be argued that in making that choice they are entering open-eyed into a relationship which entails an obligation of support. In practice, of course, the number of parents for whom such choice is seriously available is negligible.

Similarly, if parents become associated with a school which offers them a serious opportunity for participation in the determination or revision of its 'educational mission', of its guiding values and/or social code, then there is a *prima facie* case for suggesting that parents incur an obligation to support what was thus determined. As Munn points out, however, while parents are generally expected to uphold school values, 'parental involvement in identifying the values which the school will embody is rare' (Munn, 1993). Even where such opportunity is provided, however, it still constitutes no more than a *prima facie* case for a parental obligation to support: there is no shortage of argument to explain why participation in fully democratic (let along the quasi-democratic processes which are more typical of school governance even today) might be compatible with disobedience to the decisions which are the outcome of those processes (see e.g., Singer, 1973).

Nevertheless, schools themselves have become more conscious that when parental support is needed more than ever before, active support from parents is not something that will come automatically: it needs to be cultivated; it needs to be earned; it needs to be part of a richer pattern of mutual obligation and support. Hence, the notion of a 'partnership' between parents and schools.

Parents as Partners

The Plowden Report had already employed the language of partnership in 1967 — 'one of the essentials for educational advance is a closer partnership between the two parties (parents and teachers) to every child's education' (Plowden, 1967), and no doubt there are considerably earlier references, but the notion really came into its own with an added note of political realism with the publication of the Taylor Committee Report in 1977 under the title 'A New Partnership for our Schools'.

The Taylor Report was a wise and carefully balanced document, which deserved more sustained government support than it was in the end to receive. It contained in its argument and recommendations many, if not all, of the key ingredients of a proper parent–school partnership.

First, the report recognized the importance of parental support for the school. Taylor recognized the stresses which schools were under and argued: 'It is vital therefore that teachers have the support of people outside the school in the increasingly difficult task of attaining those (educational) objectives and dealing with those stresses' (para., 6.14). 'We wish to produce a structure within which every parent will have a role in supporting the school and increasing its effectiveness' (para., 5.27). Secondly, the report recognized that parents are not always as forthcoming with that support as schools would like, but pointed out that schools could do more to help parents understand what they are doing, to address parental puzzlement and actively to enlist their support. 'We believe that better forms of communication will, in time, increase parents' sense of commitment to their child's school' (para., 5.27). Thus far the Taylor Committee was on fairly well-trodden ground, but it entered more controversial territory as it developed the next step in the argument and a third element of the notion of partnership: a more equal distribution of power in the relationship between parents and school.

'If ordinary people do not, as some teachers suggest, understand what schools are trying to do,' argued Taylor, 'it is in part because they have traditionally not taken an active part in determining the educational policy of the schools' (para., 6.14). Joan Sallis, a member of the committee, expressed the full equation succinctly in the book she published shortly after the report came out: 'The case is essentially that the job schools now have to do cannot be done adequately without more support from parents and the community in general. *Support* means consent, *consent* means understanding; true *understanding* can only come from *responsibility*' (Sallis, 1977, my italics).

The Taylor Committee rejected the case put to them by, for example, the Assistant Masters' Association that, in their own terms, the curriculum 'best falls within the competence of professionally trained, experienced and practising teachers' (para., 6.13). 'We do not believe,' said Taylor, 'that these arguments justify regarding the curriculum at school level as the responsibility solely of the teachers nor are we convinced that it is right for teachers to carry this responsibility alone' (para., 6.14). And so the committee went on to argue for an increase in the power of parents vis-à-vis schools as a condition for the development of a real partnership. Parents would have stronger direct representation on governing bodies and governing bodies should have their power extended to include responsibility 'for setting the aims of the school, for considering the means by which they are pursued, for keeping under review the school's progress towards them, and for deciding upon action to facilitate such progress' (para., 6.23).

These measures, which the report recognized would only involve directly a small minority of parents, sat alongside other recommendations — a fourth ingredient of the new partnership — to do with encouraging parents' organizations and giving them access to school facilities (paras., 5.20–5.23) and ensuring that adequate arrangements are made 'to inform parents, to involve them in their children's progress and welfare, to enlist their support, and to ensure their access to the school and a teacher by reasonable arrangement' (para., 5.28). Unfortunately, however, these last relatively modest and commonsensical recommendations, which had practical bearing on relations with all parents, tended to get overshadowed by the reaction (positive and negative) to the recommendations which presaged the development of parent power, or at least power for a minority of parent activists.

Parents as Governors

Though many schools had in fact already begun to collect governors who were also parents, it was the 1980 Education Act which for the first time formally required that every school should have a governing body which included elected parents (and teachers). A little later, the 1986 Education (No 2) Act required schools to have (according to size) between two and five elected parent governors (clause 3); required governing bodies to provide parents with specified information about syllabuses etc., (clause 20) and required annual reports by governing bodies to parents at an annual meeting.

The 1986 Education Reform Act gave additional significance to these changes by providing for the extension of the powers of governing bodies e.g., through local financial management (section 33 ff). It also provided for schools to be required to admit pupils up to the level of available capacity, in effect extending albeit marginally the possibility for parental choice of school, but we shall turn to this later.

On the face of it these changes gave a new measure of power to the 75,000 parent governors who took up office in the four-year period 1986–1992. However research suggests that a proportion of these parents was bewildered by the new responsibilities and lacked the stomach for the sometimes heavily politicized conflicts in which governing bodies became embroiled. 'There is a minority which feels marginalised by manipulative heads, outranked by LEA nominated veterans, mystified by educational jargon, intimidated by paperwork' (Golby, 1993).

Let us note that in any case there were only between two and five such governors in any one school, i.e., a very small minority of the total parent body. Moreover elected parent governors remained a minority element on the governing bodies. The proposals contained in the Green Paper 'Parental Influence at School' (Department of Education and Science, 1984) that parents should elect from among their number a majority of seats on governing bodies had been rejected even by organized parents groups. There is little evidence that other parents (i.e., the vast majority of parents) felt or were significantly empowered by their presence. In most schools only a minority of parents bothered to take part in the elections for these parent governors or to attend the annual parents' meeting which was the primary vehicle for accountability between governors and parents. The Cambridge Accountability Project had already illustrated how sceptical the broad mass of parents of those who formally represented them on school bodies was (Bridges, 1981). For many parents, PTA committees and governing bodies were simply spheres of influence for what one critic called 'articulate, adroit and literate "political" people' (Seldon, 1990).

Perhaps the presence of parents as governors and their modest measure of accountability to fellow parents has contributed to school governors' and senior professional managers' awareness of parental opinion and responsiveness to it. Perhaps it is a significant ingredient among others in the changing relationship and even a developing partnership, but it hardly amounts to the meat of such partnership in the routine experience of many individual parents. For that perhaps we need to look in another direction.

Parents as Coeducators

Arguably, an important feature of a partnership in the educational process is a shared recognition of their reciprocal responsibilities and mutual respect between the two partners for the roles which each can play. It is barely sufficient for this purpose to present parents as marginal supporters in an educative task which is otherwise the exclusive responsibility of professional teachers. It also barely accords with the facts. Most children will have achieved their greatest intellectual achievement — mastering the basics of a natural language — under parental guidance before coming anywhere near a teacher. Parents must be regarded pre-school, in parallel with school and post-school as a major developmental and educative force in their children's lives. One constructive dimension of the notion of school–parent partnership in education (one neglected by the Taylor Committee) is the notion of parents as coeducators with the school — a role for parents which the schools themselves can help them to develop.

Some of the earliest ventures in this area grew out of the lessons of the Head Start programme in the United States and the realization that it was far more effective to recognize and develop the contribution that parents could make to their children's development than to seek as it were to rescue children from unsatisfactory family influence (Strom and Bernard, 1982). This shift of policy was then reflected by the nationwide beginning of Home Start in the USA in 1971 with an explicit plan to help parents to teach their own children (Croake and Glover, 1977; Gordon, 1977).

In the UK and the USA the development of parents as coeducators tended to focus on pre-school education and special education (see Wolfendale, 1983, with particular reference to special education) but already educators in both countries were coming to appreciate the benefits to children of for example programmes for the teaching of reading which had a clearly defined role for parents as well as teachers. In 1975 the highly influential Bullock Report gave its *imprimatur* to the idea of parents (usually mothers) coming into school to participate in language and beginning-reading activities which could also be extended into the home, confirming encouragingly that 'there is room for many such activities' (para., 5.37, p. 70).

Some notable projects produced impressive evidence of the success of partnership schemes (see e.g., Hewison and Tizard's 1980 report on the Haringey Reading Project or Wolfendale 1983 for a wider review). They spread rapidly throughout the UK though remained largely confined to primary education and to English and to a lesser extent maths. By 1991 a DES survey celebrated the fact that 75 per cent of all primary schools had set up a 'formal partnership' with parents to involve them in reading programmes (Department of Education and Science, 1991). In 1993 the Community Education Development Centre claimed 'a huge and convincing body of evidence and experience showing that, when teachers and parents work together in a practical partnership towards shared goals, there are real gains in pupil achievement that are both considerable and lasting' (Community Education Development Centre, 1993, p. 11).

I do not propose to enter into a detailed evaluation of this evidence, though I suggest that even allowing that some of the claims made may be excessive, it is difficult to pinpoint *any* other strategy for the improvement of children's learning with anything like the same evidence of benefit to children's progress. Moreover, though this must of course be the overriding consideration, the virtues of this kind of very practical partnership do not just end with the benefits to children's learning. Such schemes do something to restore to parents their alienated role in the education or, better, upbringing, of their own children; they are acknowledged, valued and supported in this role. At the same time the professionalism of teachers is recognized, reinforced and perhaps extended as they work in support of and in collaboration with parents rather than at a distance from them. Furthermore parents gain understanding of aspects of classrooms and education and more confidence within the school environment and in their relationship with teachers (see Liverpool LEA, 1991; and Warwickshire, LEA, 1991 both quoted extensively in Community Education Development Centre, 1993).

What is astonishing is the lack of encouragement and positive support these developments have received from government over the last fifteen years. The reason is perhaps rooted more in social and political ideology than anything else. The kind of relationship between school and parents which I have described here is an intimately collaborative one based on mutual respect, understanding and support. The Community Education Development Centre (the very title resonates with what are now political heresies!) picks out four key features:

- the sharing of power, responsibility and ownership, though not necessarily in immediately apparent ways or on an equal basis;
- a degree of mutuality, which begins with the process of listening to each other and incorporates a responsive dialogue and 'give and take' on both sides;
- shared aims and goals, based on common ground but allowing for the acknowledgement of important differences; [and]
- joint action, with parents, professionals and pupils working together to get things done. (Community Education Development Centre, 1993, p. 12)

But 'mutuality', 'responsive dialogue', the equalization of power, 'joint action' and the ethos of collaboration are a far cry from the social and political ideology which government has brought to education and indeed all other public services over the last decade. Parents are enjoined not to joint action, but to choice; not to participate, but to discriminate and to complain if they are not getting what they want. Parents are not partners in the educational enterprise but customers or clients for a service which is provided by someone else. It marks the triumph of the individualistic ethos of competition for personal self-interest over the collectivist ethos of collaboration in the interests of general welfare.

73

However, the limitation of parental involvement programmes from this point of view was articulated some years ago by Acland:

> The essence of parent participation is that parents come to school, learn about the way the school operates and through doing this become more effective so far as their children's education is concerned. It is clear that parents are there to understand and accept; they are not there to represent their own position if this conflicts with the school . . . The programmes do nothing to alter the fundamental relationship between home and school. The potential for the parents to make choices or decisions about their child's education is not increased . . . (Acland, 1979, p. 46)

Whether or not this account does justice to the best of parent–school partnership schemes, it is the pursuit of this element of *choice* in a free market of educational opportunity which now dominates the political agenda.

Parents as Customers

The reconceptualization of the parental relationship to the school as that of customer to service industry represents a radical departure from any of the other relationships described here insofar as it has been linked crucially in recent government thinking to the notion of parental choice of school. All the other relationships I have described have operated in the context in which parents and school were very largely bound to each other by the parents' accident (or of course for some people choice) of place of residence.

For the 'New Right' and eventually for the Conservative government the key conditions for the improvement of the quality of education in schools (as indeed for many other public services including health and transport) were the introduction of market conditions in which the State or in the case of education the 'LEA monopoly' (Flew, 1991) was broken; information about the character and quality of alternative service providers was available; and parents, the customers in the market place, were given the maximum possible choice.

'Choice', as David Miliband has pointed out, is meaningless in the absence of accessible alternatives. To replicate the virtues of market competition, the ERA had to establish the basis for the differentiation of educational 'products' (Miliband, 1991 p. 7). Thus, to meet the supply side of market conditions, the government promoted diversity of provision through:

- legislation to enable the establishment of City Technology Colleges;
- legislation (and a heavy promotional campaign) designed to enable and encourage schools to opt out of LEA control — followed by increasing liberality in the opportunity given to these schools to determine their own policies on e.g., discipline and, later, selection of pupils;

- an assisted places scheme designed to enable a small number of children to take up places in independent schools;
- legislation enabling schools to develop a particular specialism in e.g., the arts, mathematics or science; and
- legislation enabling parents or other bodies to set up their own schools with government support.

To satisfy the demand side of market conditions, the government reduced the constraints on parental choice of schooling. These existed mainly to ensure an economic and manageable allocation of places according to the capacity of the local service to provide, so it has not been easy for government realistically to introduce great flexibility in this area at the same time as maintaining its other commitment to take 'spare places' out of the system and to reduce unnecessary expenditure. The trouble is that to meet elasticity of demand you need elasticity of supply, and an impoverished school system does not have much of the latter. Despite, therefore, the rhetoric of choice and parent power the DES 1987 Consultation Paper on school admissions pledged only that parents 'would have the right to express a preference to the school at which they would like their child to be educated' (DES, 1987, p. 2). The 1988 Act went a step further and insisted that schools accept as many pupils as capacity allows, paving the way for potential expansion and contraction in response to market forces. The Parents' Charter declared in bold type: 'You have a right to a place in the school you want unless it is full to capacity with pupils who have a stronger claim' (DES, 1991, p. 10).

But in order for customers to exercise sensible choices they need information about the alternatives. A number of recent government measures has been designed to provide such information, even if there has been some controversy about its validity, relevance and fairness. The Parents Charter (DES, 1991) promised five 'key documents' which would provide information for parents, though it is only really the third and fourth of these that contribute directly to the market information:

- a report about parents' own child at least once a year;
- regular reports from independent inspectors;
- performance tables for all local schools;
- a prospectus or brochure about individual schools; and
- an annual report from your school governors.

Other chapters in this book will discuss the wider issues concerning the effects and appropriateness of the application of this market model to education. Some criticism focuses on the inapplicability or incompleteness of the market model in current educational conditions. The more worrying criticisms, perhaps, are those which relate to what happens when the market works 'best'.

> It is not the imperfections of the market that make it dangerous, but rather its potential to do damage where it works most effectively . . . 'Success' according to the logic established in the ERA's educational market is precisely what society requires that we avoid — namely an education system marked by (narrowly-based) excellence for an élite but sub-optimal provision for the majority of children. (Miliband, 1991, p. 13)

In this context, however, what most concerns me are the consequences of the market model for relations between parents and school. It seems to me to present a considerably impoverished view of what this relationship could and should be. For example, if parents are 'customers', then this suggests that their responsibilities are primarily to exercise informed and sensible choice of the school which will provide the educational service. But what of their own educational responsibilities and roles? As customers we expect to employ someone else to get on and do the job for us; we do not expect the plumber to turn round and remind us of the part that we have to play in fixing the pipe — that is what we pay him or her to do! Less still do we expect to contribute from our own effort to the service provided by that plumbing firm to ourselves and other customers. The trouble is, as Miliband points our again, 'under the ERA's provisions, it becomes more important for parents to battle to get their child into the best school than for them to make possible and work for the improvement in the quality of their local school' (Miliband, 1991, p. 13).

We need perhaps to distinguish here two kinds of advantage which education can bestow on children. One is a *positional* advantage which can only be achieved at someone else's expense. Thus the school which prepares its pupils (or some of its pupils) more effectively for job applications or for university entrance may bestow positional benefit to its own pupils and may affect the distribution of such benefits, but however well schools in general come to carry out this function, the net benefit to the wider population of school pupils is nil, unless the employment opportunities or chances of entering higher education themselves increase. But education also bestows other advantages which are *non*-positional and infinitely extendable. It provides insight, understanding, stimulus to interest, imagination, reflection and creativity which are viewed as intrinsically worthwhile. And these are ingredients of an educated culture from which everyone benefits the more widely and more deeply they are extended and shared (McMurtry, 1991).

The problem is that as far as parents and schools are concerned there is a considerable tension between the rational courses of action dictated by allegiance to these two perspectives on education. As a custodian of my own children's interests I must naturally seek to advance their access to the positional advantages that education can bestow even at the expense of other people's children. It suits me to have unequally distributed educational provision and advantage provided my children have the better end of the deal. At the same time, self-interest as well as altruism indicates that I and my children will benefit from a school, a community and a wider society in which the non-positional advantages of education are widely shared and celebrated — but this will, quite logically, become a distant priority to parents who can see much more sharply the immediate benefits attached to securing positional educational advantage for their child.

The consequence of this dilemma is that the more a system of schooling offers the opportunity for parents to secure positional advantage for their children, the more they will (quite rationally) exercise their custodial responsibility to secure that advantage for their own children and the less they will concern themselves with ensuring that the system provides non-positional benefits to all. The richer, educative and universally beneficial purposes of schooling will become subordinate to the narrower, self-interested function which can benefit some only at the expense of others.

The system of schooling which will most fall victim to these priorities will be one which offers a hierarchy of different schooling opportunities of just the kind which the market requires. The system of schooling best designed to secure the broader educational benefit for all will be a common and comprehensive system attached to a common curriculum, one which the competition for positional advantage is postponed for as long as possible and one in which early jockeying for positional advantage by either pupils or parents is actively discouraged.

In such a context the rules can be constructed so that parents' natural and proper desire to act in the interest of their own children become rationally directed to efforts which benefit the wider community (as well). They are thus partners with the school and with other parents in a genuinely educational enterprise more than manipulators of the school system and in competition with other parents for the sake of the positional advantage of their own children. Of course no one should be so naive as to imagine that this second element of the parental educational enterprise will entirely disappear. But we do not need deliberately to construct market mechanisms in education perfectly designed to maximize the narrowly self-interested pursuit of positional advantage at the expense of the more broadly socially (including self) interested pursuit of a widely educative and educated community.

Conclusion

The positive notions that we were looking at earlier — of parents as partners with teachers, of parents as coeducators — are incompletely worked out. Interesting consideration has begun as to the value of some more or less formal 'contract' between parents and schools setting out their mutual obligations (see Tomlinson, 1991, for a useful discussion of these). There is widespread acknowledgment that if parents are to take an active part in the education of their own children, then some will need considerably more support than others in the process, and schemes have been initiated in the area of parent education. There is recognition for example that schemes which teach reading to illiterate parents alongside their children may be one way of breaking the persistent cycle of illiteracy. There remains a great deal to be done in defining and achieving the most appropriate distribution of power between parents and schools and the mechanisms for its operation. But, as we have seen, the evidence of the effects of these sorts of development is impressive. Independently of these consequentialist considerations, there will be many parents who sense in these developments rather than in the market mechanisms a healthier presentation of their role in a relationship not just with the teachers and the school but with the child whose welfare must be in the end the focus of all these endeavours.

References

ACLAND, H. (1979) 'Does parent involvement matter?', in WILSON, M. *Social and Education Research in Action*, London, Longmans/Open University.

AULD, R. (1976) *William Tyndale Junior and Infant Schools Public Enquiry: A report to the ILEA*, London, Inner London Education Authority.

BRIDGES, D. (1981) *It's the ones who never turn up that you really want to see: The 'problem' of the non-attending parent'*, in ELLIOTT, J. et al., *School Accountability*, London, Grant MacIntyre.

CENTRAL ADVISORY COUNCIL FOR EDUCATION (England) (1963) *Half Our Future* (The Newsom Report), London, HMSO.

CENTRAL ADVISORY COUNCIL FOR EDUCATION (England) (1967) *Children and their Primary Schools* (Plowden Report), Vol. 1, London, HMSO.

COMMUNITY EDUCATION DEVELOPMENT CENTRE (1993) *Parents as Co-educators*, Coventry, Community Education Development Centre.

CROAKE, J. and GLOVER, K. (1977) 'A history and evaluation of parent education', *The Family Coordinator*, 2, 2, pp. 151–8.

DEPARTMENT OF EDUCATION AND SCIENCE (1977) *A new partnership for our schools*, Report of the Taylor Committee, London, HMSO.

DEPARTMENT OF EDUCATION AND SCIENCE (1984) *Parental Influence at School*, Cmnd. 9242, London, HMSO.

DEPARTMENT OF EDUCATION AND SCIENCE (1987) *Admission of Pupils to Maintained Schools*, (Consultation Paper) London, Department of Education and Science.

DEPARTMENT OF EDUCATION AND SCIENCE (1991) *The Parents Charter*, London, Department of Education and Science.

DEPARTMENT OF EDUCATION AND SCIENCE (1991) *The teaching and learning of reading in primary schools*, London, HMSO.

DEPARTMENT FOR EDUCATION AND WELSH OFFICE (1992) *Choice and Diversity: a new framework for schools*, London, HMSO.

'Education Act', 1980, London, HMSO.

'Education (No 2) Act', 1986, London, HMSO.

'Education Reform Act', 1988, London, HMSO.

ELLIOTT, J., BRIDGES, D., EBBUTT, D., GIBSON, R. and NIAS, J. (1981) *School Accountability*, London, Grant MacIntyre.

FLEW, A. (1991) 'Education services: Independent competition or maintained monopoly?', in GREEN, D.G. (Ed) *Empowering Parents*, London, Inner London Education Authority, Health and Welfare Unit.

GOLBY, M. (1993) 'Parents as school Governors', in MUNN, P. (Ed) *Parents and Schools*, London, Routledge.

GORDON, I. (1977) 'Parent education and parent involvement: Retrospect and prospect', in *Childhood Education*, 54, 2, pp. 71–8.

GREEN, D.G. (Ed) (1991) *Empowering Parents*, London, Inner London Education Authority, Health and Welfare Unit.

HEWISON, J. and TIZARD, J. (1980) 'Parental involvement and reading attainment', *British Journal of Educational Psychology*, 50, pp. 209–15.

LIVERPOOL LOCAL EDUCATION AUTHORITY (1991) *The Liverpool policy on parental involvement in education*, Liverpool, Liverpool City Council.

MCMURTRY J. (1991) 'Education and the market model', *Journal of Philosophy of Education*, 25, 2, pp. 209–17.

MILIBAND, D. (1991) 'Markets, politics and education', *Education and Training Paper 3*, London, Institute for Public Policy Research.

MUNN, P. (1993) (Ed) *Parents and schools*, London, Routledge.

SALLIS, J. (1977) *School Managers and Governors: Taylor and After*, London, Ward Lock.

SELDON, A. (1990) *Capitalism*, Oxford, Basil Blackwell.

SINGER, P. (1973) *Democracy and Disobedience*, Oxford, Clarendon Press.

STROM, R.D. and BERNARD, H.W. (1982) *Educational Psychology*, Monterey, California, Brooks/Cole.

TAYLOR REPORT (1977) *A New Partnership for our Schools*, London, HMSO.

TOMLINSON, S. (1991) 'Home School Partnerships', in *Teachers and Parents*, Education and Training Paper 7, London, Institute for Public Policy Research.

WARWICKSHIRE LOCAL EDUCATION AUTHORITY (1991) *Reporting to Parents*, Warwick, Warwickshire County Council.

WOLFENDALE, S. (1983) *Parental Participation in Children's Development and Education*, London, Gordon and Breach.

Chapter 8

Business Sponsorship in Schools: A Changing Climate

Peter Roberts

A leading supermarket chain claims to have given 3,000 computers and some 10,000 other items to schools as a result of their scheme which offers one voucher for every £25 spent in their stores. These vouchers can be exchanged for items of equipment for hard-pressed schools. The commercial success of this scheme which has already been repeated is currently being taken up by several other retailers nationwide. These firms clearly perceive that both public-relations benefits and substantial profits lie in children being encouraged to urge their parents to make purchases so that they can take the vouchers to school. In another current scheme schools are being urged to install Coca-Cola machines to help them to 'balance their budgets'.

Are these examples just the latest trend in a continuing and relatively harmless series of marketing ploys aimed at children? Do they suggest the emergence of a new aspect of business sponsorship in school? How concerned should we be that children in schools are seen as fair targets for sales promotions such as these? By what criteria should we assess whether business influence upon schools is exploitive rather than beneficent and supportive?

To take a contrasting example, BP have recently celebrated twenty-five years of commitment to their 'Schools Link Scheme' which has over the years developed relationships with over 200 schools by means of link officers. The scheme has promoted the teaching of science and technology, the secondment of both teachers and industrialists and European work-experience exchanges. It was back in 1981 when their personnel director declared 'our primary social responsibility will continue to be towards education as we believe that the most important resources a nation possesses are the skills and knowledge of its people'.

I believe that it is important to examine carefully the motives of both business and schools as we explore the wide range of business sponsorship in education today. A helpful start might be to recognize a 'spectrum of motivation' from the sharply commercial at one end to the genuine concern for the quality of education at the other. I shall argue that if the strong and welcome development of the 'Business Education Partnership' movement is to fulfil expectations then it is essential for both partners to be clear, honest and explicit about their aims and rigorous in developing and applying the criteria of their business–education liaison policies.

If we take the examples quoted above the contrast between these two approaches is striking in several respects. The second arises from a company policy commitment, which is long-term and explicit, to enhancing the quality of education in relatively broad terms. Benefit to the company itself would be limited and indirect and could hardly be translated into obvious commercial profit. There will have undoubtedly been many schools, teachers and children who will have gained substantially from this commitment over many years.

On the other hand the first example is blatant. 'We would not do a promotion like this if it was not profitable for us. The fact that we are doing it a second time round must mean something', the promoter is quoted as saying. There is not even the pretence of altruism here and in fact the company does very nicely from a scheme which brings in £125,000 in grocery sales to the company for every high-specification 'donated' computer. Another retailer's scheme will produce £10,000 in till receipts for every £500 worth of books given to primary schools (a sum which will not go far in today's school library, by the way).

A number of serious objections can be made to company promotions of this type. Firstly, they are dishonest. The promoters are posing as benefactors of schools when in fact they are exploiting them as closed markets. Few schools will turn away the proffered vouchers though some may do so for reasons of the time and effort involved in collecting them. They will frequently be seen as a bonus backed by reputable high-street retailers. Furthermore there may be some schools, urged on by their PTAs, who will throw themselves wholeheartedly into the business of voucher accumulation with class competitions and rewards for the most successful collectors. Children will be pressurizing their parents to make extra purchases and doing the work of the company promoter. The school will be placed in the position of being seen to promote a particular company. There is also the issue of divisiveness as schools in middle-class areas will be far more likely to benefit from such schemes where spending power and selective shopping are at a premium.

It may be that to some parents and teachers these arguments themselves may sadly seem no longer relevant. There are schools where the realities of their inadequate budgets mean that for some time they have had to fund-raise in whatever ways they can in order to provide basic books and materials. The number of schools which find themselves able to devote their fund-raising efforts exclusively to providing desirable 'extras' is declining. Driven by necessity such schools have found themselves compelled to compromise the criteria they would much have preferred to maintain. For example they may now feel they should accept direct company advertising in school corridors or the selling of all manner of unhealthy confectionery in their school shops for the sake of the income generated. These schools are vulnerable to the more exploitive commercial schemes, relying as they do upon the basic underfunding of the education service and the failure of statutory provision to guarantee an adequate baseline of resources.

A strong case may be made out by severely underfunded schools for seeking additional funding by whatever means they can but it is a different matter elsewhere. Well supported schools in more affluent areas may benefit hugely from the business professionals on their governing and parent bodies but the risks for these schools of compromising their stance as impartial educators are perhaps greater, as one or two nationally publicized excesses have shown.

At this point we should perhaps remind ourselves that there never was a time when the state system of education was adequately funded and the funding variations from one local education authority to another have always been wide and fluctuating. However, the steady erosion of the powers of local education authorities and the pressure towards grant-maintained status have combined to reduce sharply the checks that used to be built into the education system, however imperfectly, to create a certain degree of equity in funding.

There is little to mitigate the harsh climate in which schools must make judgments about whether they are prepared to embrace all aspects of the new market in education. It is inevitable that there will be considerable variation in the decisions schools arrive at about what is and what is not acceptable practice. It is profoundly important however that the issues are faced and addressed and that the response is not simply a shrug of resignation as each new commercial initiative or pressure comes along.

Most schools welcome the opportunities and scope that LMS has brought them to enhance their resources in a multitude of ways and very many are already exercising great inventiveness to maximize the benefit to school facilities and learning resources. However this does not require an uncritical acceptance of a new commercial ethic. Rather it requires schools to recognize and explore honestly and carefully the implications of the 'education market' upon their fundamental responsibilities to children. At issue are the values the school declares in its 'Aims and Objectives' or 'Mission Statement'.

One of these responsibilities must be to provide a learning environment for children which is free from manipulation whether social, political or commercial. To allow an individual company or brand name to be exclusively promoted within a school must surely infringe this basic responsibility; to promote two or three companies equally would not seem to be significantly different. But other criteria are also relevant, such as the age of the children. If a company sponsors a sixth-form conference, for example, the risk of commercial exploitation most would judge to be relatively slight. The comparative maturity of the students and the limited extent of their active involvement in any promotion become significant factors. However should one company over a period of time gain very regular and exceptional access even to more mature students one could argue that the cumulative effect would be invidious. What used to be termed the school's 'hidden curriculum' is susceptible to 'drip-feed' influence. All potential sponsorship needs thorough and careful consideration therefore.

In terms of the curriculum it should be obvious that enterprise education should be balanced by consumer education and that the school canteen and tuck shop should not be contradicting daily the messages of the health-education programme! However the provision of unbiased learning materials is another basic responsibility which presents more complex questions to schools. Few would argue that there can be no place for any learning materials which companies donate to schools but such materials always require shrewd professional scrutiny before they are used and some will require an explicit 'health warning' to students. Other examples should be considered unacceptable even by the most impoverished school for their blatant partiality. There are many examples of thoroughly well-balanced, high-quality materials provided free of charge by companies to schools but sponsorship of learning materials should always be an especially sensitive area. Imagine a scenario when main National Curriculum (NC) textbooks in food and nutrition were to be sponsored by, let us say, MacDonald's restaurants UK!

Most schools are not naive or inexperienced in these respects but there are undoubtedly new pressures and dangers which accompany the financial responsibilities they now have to carry. Some promotions are being devised with subtlety and plausibility and require sharp scrutiny to prevent the compromising of the essential trust placed in schools by parents and children. The very many companies who genuinely and generously support schools and the education service as a whole would have no difficulty with schools applying more rigorous criteria and many would indeed encourage such an approach. Most schools can point to firms in their locality who offer them support in a multitude of ways with little obvious or direct benefit in return except in terms of what we may call long-term enlightened self-interest.

One of the striking developments of recent years, enhanced by the Technical and Vocational Education Initiative (TVEI), has been the rich diversity of local business–education sponsorship. The range includes imaginative ways of giving schools 'person support' where examples include mock interviews, managers running conferences, making presentations, acting as consultants or mentors and the development of a vast array of curriculum projects from the one-off to those which become an integrated part of schemes of work. Over the years work-experience and work-shadowing placements have become much better prepared, supervised and followed up. Work experience has become part of the curriculum and also one component in a continuing dialogue between firms and schools which develops their relationship.

All forms of 'person support' represent substantial costs to, and commitment from, companies but benefits are reciprocal. Companies can come to perceive benefit for their staff-training programmes in encouraging their managers and employees to work in schools where there are excellent opportunities for developing presentation skills, group leadership and, increasingly, mentoring. In addition to the benefits of good public relations, many firms are seeking to promote a positive and caring image in their local community. It has been my experience that the deeper the business-education partnership the greater the mutuality of benefit becomes, sometimes in ways which could not have been anticipated. Not least of the drawbacks of a self-seeking, ex-ploitive approach is that perceptions are confined to what may be 'got out of' the relationship; where nothing is freely given or committed; returns must inevitably be limited.

There is a significant number of large companies who have sustained impressive sponsorship programmes for education encompassing curriculum projects and materials supporting educational organizations, conferences, publications and research. There is a number of major charitable trusts and foundations sponsorship whose has enabled key curriculum developments and initiatives. Nuffield is an example which immediately springs to mind. The trustees of these foundations apply principles based upon traditions of public service, some to the point where no form of recognition or publicity is looked for; they often have particular commitments or enthusiasms. Some are keen to ensure that their pump-priming initiatives are taken up by publicly funded institutions.

In my own experience one of the Sainsbury Family Charitable Trusts responded with imagination and generosity to a proposal based upon raising the low aspirations of pupils, especially girls, and improving the relevance of education to social and economic circumstances. The trustees wished to work with an education authority which had the determination and capacity to implement and sustain a county-wide programme arising out of the work undertaken in the pilot schools. Over seven years the Suffolk Schools Indus-try Project (SSIP) has directly benefited ninety-six schools and enabled 139 projects involving 307 companies (Suffolk County Council, 1993). Schemes like this one make a genuine and long-lasting difference to the quality of education, as the learning projects were evaluated, case studies published and disseminated and innovative methods of teaching and training in conjunction with local firms were developed to become a continuing part of the schools' curriculum in many instances.

The SSIP and other similar schemes have demonstrated that a reservoir of goodwill and a positive enthusiasm to support local schools exists in the commercial world. Local companies particularly are keen to contribute exper-tise and resources to well-planned school projects. One project will often lead to another; relationships develop into partnerships. At the local level there are many schools and firms which have a rich experience of this process. In Suffolk and elsewhere employer-recognition awards celebrate exceptional con-tributions within thriving local networks. Frequently it is the small companies which are making a real difference to the neighbourhood schools. Proportion-ately their contribution may well be much greater than that of national com-panies. One frustration can be the constraints placed upon the local branches which have a policy in all major respects determined centrally by national head office. Banks for example often appear to have little discretion to support local schools. Their national schemes tend to relate directly to capturing future customers via, for example, school banks and money-management resource packs. Marks and Spencer is one company which has proved that highly centralized policy need not restrict local initiative.

Particular uncertainty arises when government has tried to steer company sponsorship to promote their own political agenda as was the case with city technology colleges. A majority of companies was not prepared to sponsor such a restricted and circumscribed approach to the development of technology teaching. It will be interesting to see whether their latest strategy of 'sponsor governors' will fare any better. Under this scheme schools successful under the 'Technology Schools Initiative' can appoint 'sponsor governors' so long as they are, or become grant-maintained or voluntary-aided! Additional DFE money will be available to match money provided by this new type of governor. In other words can local schools attract the sponsorship which national government failed to do?

There is considerable evidence that many industrialists and businessmen have a wider perspective. They may either look for ways of supporting broadly-based curriculum projects and initiatives which can be effectively disseminated, such as the 'Technology Enhancement Project' run by the Engineering Council, or back consortia of schools within a structured national framework. A less ideologically-bound government would be looking for ways to stimulate initiatives along these lines.

Just as companies may give their name to specific building developments, sponsor the minibus, provide furniture or equipment at cost price, or make their facilities available, so they are likely to be receptive to well-researched proposals for supporting individual schools or consortia without strings attached. In the early days of business–education links the concept of 'twinning' grew up but one reason we hear less today of this approach is that some companies are not keen on the exclusiveness implicit in this.

Both firms and individual managers have found satisfaction from extended commitment to schools. Schemes such as 'Neighbourhood Engineers' have encouraged longer-term relationships on an open-ended basis where there are no preconceived expectations. Sponsorship of events and projects arises naturally from such linking as needs and opportunities come to be more clearly identified and understood. The rapid growth of teacher placements in business has brought further impetus to joint projects and there are some examples of business secondments to schools, though not as yet very many. In addition increasing numbers of firms actively encourage their employees to become school governors (e.g., the Trustee Savings Bank claims 190 governors, most having been recruited over the last year).

Schools for their part have largely moved away from any simplistic expectation that an appeal to local firms will produce cheques. Financial grants may still be made but probably less frequently and usually in support of a carefully negotiated scheme with specific objectives, for example, improving information-technology (IT) skills in young people. Even in the depths of a long recession when cash is scarce and comparatively few firms are recruiting school leavers many schools can report that the tangible support that they have come to rely upon has largely been maintained at a similar level; in some cases it has even been extended. Companies are prepared to commit managers' time and other resources to sponsor school-based projects which have clearly worked-out objectives, action plans and success criteria. Most commonly the initiative comes from the school because firms wish to know where they can contribute most effectively and few industrialists and businessmen are sufficiently aware of the current school context. This is hardly a state of affairs for which they can be blamed given the scale of the upheavals within the education service of recent years!

A recent investigation into Business Sponsorship in Education carried out in Swindon shows that the concept of obligation to serve the community still survives in many firms and flourishes in some:

> Business is being charitable and having a community responsibility. It will be another decade before that is understood. It is not being paternalistic but generally trying to be collaborative, and that is a strange thing for the outside world actually to grasp and work with because the traditional view of business is that it is about profit and not about the finer points of education or charitable action. There will always be a gap and a growing number of companies are trying to be part of the new grouping of companies that are saying we have got to get closer alongside people rather than impose our views on them. We're not helped by government because government keep saying 'bring business solutions in' so when we arrive at the doorstep of the school there is the expectation that they are going to get talked at, told what to do as opposed to being worked with in a collaborative way. (Bridges, 1993, p. 15)

The Swindon report provides further evidence of issues we have been considering.

Few companies even tried to explain the benefits of support for schools in terms of e.g., improvement in sales. Most gave reasons to do with relationships with staff and the local community. If we are to accept what we are told at its face value we would have to recognize that an important part of company motivation is not to do with calculable benefit to the company but to do with a wish or even a simple moral obligation to contribute something to the community. In the end the most convincing evidence for companies of the wisdom of their investment in schools may well be evidence of the benefits of their investment to children's education rather than evidence of its benefits to the bottom line of the company accounts.

Though some businesses still look for direct promotion others simply look for public acknowledgment and recognition not as benefactors but as identified partners:

The philanthropy of the 1970s and the early '80s is almost dead and what is coming into it now is a much more business-like approach . . . we want to be identified as being involved with . . . so that it is clear that we have a stake in your future. (ibid.)

What was significant too in the study was that companies expect schools to have 'a clear policy or set of principles which [they believe] in and could be open about' and to be well organized with clearly identified staff roles so that quality control can be 'jointly managed by schools and the companies'.

There is substantial evidence to suggest that businesses which invest in schools see the benefits as being indirect and long-term. Alongside the attraction of giving the companies a positive image in the local community, of perhaps facilitating future recruitment and giving development opportunities to their staff there are modern versions of the philanthropy of earlier years. There is still the satisfaction of helping young people to develop their life skills not just their vocational skills by offering company support not only to schools' career programmes but to their personal and social education programmes. Most adults other than teachers genuinely enjoy sharing their expertise and experience with children and students and increasingly the plethora of various forms of business sponsorship give them opportunities to do so. The current growth of the Business Education Partnership movement is providing the framework and support for this more enlightened approach and enables the broad-based strategy which many employers favour.

For example there are now emerging in particular areas more sophisticated 'Compacts'. The recession prevented Compacts in their initial form from delivering the key ingredient of jobs to student 'achievers' who had reached agreed standards of attendance, punctuality, and completion of courses. New Compacts are now emerging based upon local collaboration between schools and employers whereby a wider range of student goals covering records of achievement, individual action plans, and NC achievements are rewarded by a 'portfolio' of sponsorships, bursaries, enhanced training credits, guaranteed interviews and particular rewards, such as sports-centre passes, tokens and travel vouchers. The main point is that such Compacts will be locally devised, ownership will be guaranteed and developments determined by local needs and aspirations.

Where there is genuine partnership between business and school then there is a guarantee of local control. Where schools produce development plans which have their objectives, priorities and success criteria clearly spelled out they will find themselves much better protected both from overt and more insidious exploitation, which is more likely to find opportunities when schools have not clearly worked out and declared their aims and their stance. Responsible business will not just respect but require this clarity of planning and I also see little evidence that there are many businesses who wish to promote one school at the expense of its neighbours despite government pressure in this direction.

Peter Roberts

Experience shows that most firms need little persuasion to see schools as partners in a shared enterprise to develop young people to become effective adults, not mere consumers or producers. The need for unthinking assembly-line workers which led to cynicism in the educational world is steadily declining as the technology revolution accelerates and more enlightened management practices such as 'Investors in People' gain ground.

Schools should be encouraged therefore to maintain a positive proactive stance, to affirm their values with confidence and recognize that they have every reason to work for genuine partnership with business. This has nothing to do with being passive agents for commercialism. As the 'Investors in People' movement strongly supported by the TECs is currently showing there are long-established strengths of the education business which companies themselves are increasingly keen to share. Both business and education are coming to realize their common interest and demonstrate it in practical schemes the impact of which can prove to be strikingly beneficial to young people.

References

BRIDGES, D. (1993) 'What's in it for us?', *Education 2000 Swindon*, UEA School of Education.
SUFFOLK COUNTY COUNCIL (1993) *Suffolk Schools Industry Project: Final Report.*

Chapter 9

Pied Piper Revisited

Sheila Harty

Legend holds that 700 years ago in the medieval town of Hamelin, Germany, a mysterious piper dressed in gay colours spirited away the town's children along with a plague of rats. However, as with legends, nothing is certain. Some say the man wasn't a piper and the rats were fictitious. The Brothers Grimm may have added these elements to their fairy tale in 1812 to give the piper a motive. His motive was always the missing element. What is certain is that throughout the fourteenth century local legend spoke of 130 young people disappearing from Hamelin. As early as 1300, a stained glass window in a city church showed a man in colourful clothes surrounded by a group of children. No written account appears in town chronicles until a 1384 entry that read: 'It is 10 years since our children left.'

Modern interpretations vary. Some say a priest organized a children's crusade to the Holy Land. Others say the great plague of rats wiped out the young. The more believable story is that recruiters from the Baltic region of eastern Europe led off the young to colonize their territories. Surnames from that region today are similar to those from Hamelin. Historians explain the absence of any written record of this event for 100 years and also provide the piper's motive. They suggest that the children were sold by the town to the Baltic recruiter. In those times, many orphans, illegitimate children, and delinquents became a burden on societies that were either unwilling or unable to accommodate them. The town could have been too ashamed to register the event of their barter in any official record. Indeed, the town may have sold out their children to the highest bidder.

The Piper Returns

In researching an update to my 1979 report *Hucksters in the Classroom* and my 1985 report *The Corporate Pied Piper*, I became distressed. News from the frontlines of the big business of education is worse. Corporations wanting access to the youth market of 50 million children in USA schools were courted by a recent ad in *Advertising Age*:

> Kids spend 40 per cent of each day in the classroom where traditional advertising can't reach them. Now, you can enter the classroom through custom-made learning materials created with your specific marketing objectives in mind.

Another ad in the same issue of *Ad Age* was placed by the Modern Talking Picture Service Inc. The ad shows a kid dressed as an executive with the caption, 'Reach him at the office', and continues: 'His first day job is kindergarten. Modern can put your sponsored educational materials in the lesson plan'.

The worst part of this new evidence of marketing to school children is that these hucksters are not corporations. They are intermediaries — pimps for corporations, if I may, or educational consultants, if you prefer. That ad was placed by Lifetime Learning Systems Inc., a Connecticut-based firm that contracts its expertise in curriculum and marketing with corporations to reach that profitable youth market specifically in the classroom. Lifetime can boast of producing 'Count Your Chips', a math unit for grades 2–4, for the National Potato Board and the Snack Food Association. Lifetime also produced an educational kit for General Mills on its Gushers fruit snacks for use with lessons plans on volcanoes. For the Bic Corporation, Lifetime produced an elementary school writing programme with its pen's logo on worksheets and posters.

Modern produced a geography unit for Holiday Inn Worldwide Inc., a peace-education curriculum for the jeans maker, Marrithe and Francois Girbaud Co., as well as a bill-of-rights teaching package for the tobacco manufacturer, Phillip Morris Companies Inc. Though once tots in toyland, school children have clearly become mavens of the market place.

Whittle Communications' Channel One

Recent interest in the hucksters issue was sparked by the first new element in direct marketing to schools for decades, albeit the worst yet. Channel One is a slick twelve-minute news programme with two minutes of commercials broadcast to 12,000 middle schools and high schools in the United States. Produced and marketed by Whittle Communications, a commercial fever in the brain of Christopher Whittle of Knoxville (Tennessee), Channel One was launched in 1990 and now reaches 8 million students.

Whittle offers each school a three-year contract that exchanges $50,000 worth of satellite dish, video-cassette recorder, and 25-inch colour-television monitors for each classroom for the promise for showing Channel One to 90 per cent of the students throughout 90 per cent of the school year. Whittle charges advertisers $157,000 per each 30-second commercial. Annual revenues for Whittle Communications in 1993 were close to $120 million. Recently, Whittle has asked subscribers for permission to extend commercial time to 2.5

minutes for the 1993-4 school year. Some states, such as California, North Carolina, and Texas, have attempted to ban Channel One from its schools. Although New York state succeeded, Whittle Communications has invested in heavily lobbying the state legislature to reverse the ban.

Because the *Hucksters* and *Corporate Pied Piper* reports are pre-Whittle, education reformers and critics alike may consider my data dated. *Hucksters* reflects statistics, quotes, and examples of commercial and industrial encroachment on USA schools from research in the late 1970s. The *Pied Piper* report, researched in the mid-1980s, reflects the marketing practices of multinational corporations toward schools in Europe and the Third World. The examples may change, but the motives of vested interests remain the same; as do our principles in objection.

Marketing to kids is everywhere: company magazines (Burger King), discount clubs (Delta Airlines), corporate summer camps (Hyatt Hotels), kid vacations (Carnival Cruise Lines), theme parks (Anheuser-Busch), credit cards (Discover). But marketing to school children is egregiously different and particularly unconscionable precisely because the classroom is a captive audience of minors in a tax-supported public institution with a pedagogical responsibility. Business interests point to the crisis in public education as the motive for their initiatives. But corporate America is not saving the education crisis, but exploiting it.

To continue this dialogue, I have excerpted *The Corporate Pied Piper* and refer readers as well to more recent reports, and others still incubating, listed in the references.

Twentieth-century's Pied Piper

Today, educators have sold out our children to the modern-day Pied Piper — Big Business. Schools have allowed business interests to access the classroom as a captive audience of minors. And not just school children but their teachers as well are being led astray by the flash of colour and the sound of jingles from market advertisers. The attraction of free multicolour, multimedia curricula materials produced by commercial and industrial sponsors are the modern equivalent of the Piper's seduction.

In the United States

The best sales pitch ever advanced in USA schools was the Cheeseborough Ponds' advertising campaign which promoted Q-Tips cotton swabs through an art contest aimed at primary grades. Student entries for paintings and construction models had to use Q-Tips as the paintbrush, the glue applicator, or the construction material. Prizes amounted to $40,000 worth of USA savings bonds for four winners per grade.

Teachers' chances at a sweepstake drawing were increased with each student who entered the contest. The winning teacher was awarded a paid 'art experience' for two in either Athens, Cairo, or Florence. Now that's guaranteed to sell Q-Tips. Multiply the number of cotton swabs needed to construct a model car (nearly 500) by the number of students in an art class and the number of schools participating. That's a considerable sales figure, plus public-relations benefits.

In Sweden

The best sales pitch reported from schools outside the United States was from the Russell Company in Sweden. What is significant about their promotional strategy was how it circumvented the prohibition against commercial sponsors in Swedish schools. The exception to the rule is for sports organizations — and then only with the headteacher's permission.

The Russell Company approached headteachers throughout Sweden to enlist the participation of students in yo-yo competitions held at local shopping centres. Special yo-yos were required to enter the competition to give everyone an equal chance. These yo-yos carried brand names and advertising logos of Coca Cola, Fanta, and Sprite. The winners of the competition received expensive bicycles, and all competitors were served Coca Cola.

In Malaysia

The best classroom sales pitch reported from the Third World was from the Nestlé Company. The company launched a promotional campaign in the schools of Malaysia in apparent attempt to counteract adverse publicity and decreased sales after the worldwide boycott of Nestlé's products. The significance of its ploy was how they commandeered education authorities to mandate it. NUPRO or Nutritional Products Ltd., as the company subsidiary is known in Malaysia, sponsored nationwide cookery competitions for all secondary schools.

School-district and state-level cook-offs, mandated by the National Ministry of Education, led to a national cookery competition. A circular addressed to the headmasters of each school was signed by the deputy director of education in each state. The announcement explained that every school that teaches home economics was required to participate in the competition with at least two teams of students. The competition also required that all dinner recipes include at least two Maggie products (a Nestlé's brand) and dessert recipes include Nestlé's sweetened condensed milk. And the prizes? Winners at local, state, and national competitions all received Nestlé's products.

Still, cotton swabs, yo-yos, and food stuffs are sufficiently benign. Other company promotional gimmicks are less so. Students have received simulated uranium pellets mounted under plastic on annotated postcards. Introducing the 'Powerful Pellet,' such postcards were distributed to local schools by Public Service Company of Indiana, a USA electric utility. This offensive strategy was timed for the company's proposed construction of a nuclear power plant in the community.

Kids for Sale

Corporate advertising appears around the world in children's comic books and colouring books, on toys, T-shirts, lunch boxes, and radios. Everything in the child's world — even contests and games — is a marketing vehicle. Business interests have already coopted commercial television, children's publishing, and sports. Marketing the products, images, and issues of business has become a problem now in the schools.

How have these trade and manufacturing interests hijacked educational systems as vehicles for commercial propaganda? Educators, as a rule, have accommodated the practice. They are caught in a bind between not having sufficient or quality instructional resources nor sufficient time to review the business philanthropy proffered. Parents, as a rule, are more outraged. They can evaluate commercial material more objectively and are also more personally concerned with its effects on their children.

One parent's complaint about a comic book her daughter brought home from school is representative. The comic from an electric company presented a false trade-off between conservation and pollution. Mrs Cross of Indiana USA noted 'the comic's presence in my daughter's classroom with no critical discussion of its point of view and with no counter materials available infuriate me.' Her further criticisms highlight all the issues:

- the bland acceptance of commercial material by the school personnel because it's free;
- the use of consumers' money to distribute the utility company's propaganda;
- the lack of similar opportunity for opposing views to address the classroom audience; and
- the ignorance of most parents about their children even having such material.

Mrs Cross spoke for most parents, consumers, and conscientious educators when she summed up the cultural and intellectual problems of such corporate practices:

Children are exploited over and over again by innumerable commercial groups. Parents must train their children to be critical and to rebel against this manipulation. But what can we do about the parents who are not motivated to do that? Their children are walking around with McDonald's backpacks, Coca Cola hats, and thinking that a little air pollution won't hurt you.

Who then is responsible for monitoring business involvement in the schools? Are there criteria to help teachers evaluate commercial materials? Do legislative or administrative protections exist to curb marketing excess? What is the business of business? Whose needs are commercial materials serving? If advertising should be kept to a minimum, who decides? Can brand names be used? Are some products more acceptable than others? Who determines acceptability?

A Strategy of Effective Marketing

The marketing strategy that focuses on children in schools differs from classical market monopolies. In 'horizontal concentration', one firm acquires others in the same product field and thus eliminates competition in that market. In 'vertical concentration', one firm acquires control over both production and distribution and thus eliminates related business opportunities.

In contrast, what we might call 'diagonal concentration' describes a corporate strategy that targets a particular market audience, rather than a product field or commercial process. Women have been targets, as has the Third World. Children are an even more desirable target because of their proven ability to influence adult-purchasing behaviour. Consequently, the child market is attractive to corporations that sell fast foods, toys, soft drinks, sweets, sports equipment, clothing, and entertainment items.

How do we distinguish between education and advertising or between public service and propaganda? The distinction between commercial advertising and editorializing can be thinly veiled. Advertising itself has evolved rapidly from product information to sensate persuasion, to the creation of artificial needs, and recently to newer variations such as institutional advertising, image advertising, and issue advertising. Instead of promoting specific products, corporations are now promoting broader social issues. The result is that corporate public-relations departments can disguise their commercial intent under benign educational motives. Thus, issue advertising is used to argue a company's position on current public controversies.

As a result, firms with significant access to capital can skew social, economic, or political debate through sustained campaigns in the schools, in the community, or through the media. This trend away from specific product claims relieves firms of laboratory or statistical proof for their statements and leaves them less vulnerable to accusations of false or misleading advertising. Thus, corporate advertising, buried in a discussion of issues, entraps educators in the manœuvres of language and the camouflage of public relations.

Curricula materials from business interests are inherently deceptive because they purport to be educational while disguising their promotional intent. As long as we defer to this masquerade, business interests will continue to avoid accountability. Business involvement in education is a form of propaganda that furthers the goals of a commercial culture. Under business' tutelage, knowledge becomes the means to an end — quantitative, pragmatic, and marketable. The result is an anti-intellectual emphasis that creates a trade school mentality to secure jobs and a consumptionist drive to purchase status goods.

Who Pays the Piper?

Corporations assert public-service motives for their sponsorship of educational materials, but such contributions are not without self-interest. Business dollars spent on education are a sound tax deductible investment in future customers and employees, as well as a prime public-relations opportunity. But money spent on indoctrinating students and seducing teachers diverts capital away from more critical responsibilities, such as waste management, quality control, retooling, and efficiency. Education initiatives are an escape from business' direct obligations as producer and employer — fair wages, safety standards, training, and health coverage. In lieu, our kids are commercially hip, but products continue into planned obsolescence and employees into underpensioned futures.

Conditions within the school system invite this corporate philanthropy, primarily the underfinancing of education. Overworked teachers who lack adequate curricula resources have legitimate needs. Such teachers accept industry handouts with gratitude and often without sufficient scrutiny or suspicion. In the United States, only 1 per cent of school budgets is spent on curricula materials, although 90 per cent of classroom time is spent using materials. Curricula budgets in all countries are eclipsed by teachers' salaries and by overheads for property and maintenance. Consequently, schools look to the business community to underwrite their needs. In response, multinational corporations and native industry have responded to an open market.

Drawing on private monies to underwrite curricula materials is contrary to the structure and principles of democratic, tax-supported, public education. Curricula materials, like teachers' salaries, should come from public monies without intervention from commercial interests. Would it be acceptable for one teacher's salary to be paid by a single corporation? Would we trust what is taught, for example, by an Exxon fellow or a Texaco teacher? The distribution of private funds for curricula materials instead merely spreads the other more obvious investment. Profit-making, product-producing, private interests have no business paying teachers' salaries or producing curricula materials.

The irony of increased corporate involvement in USA education is that federal support of education was removed on the grounds that local support was preferred to retain local community values. Yet the corporate parents of increasingly popular 'Adopt-a-School' programmes in the United States are often multinationals like Coca Cola, AT&T, Chevron, and McDonald's. These corporations adopt a local or needy school and involve themselves in providing management and technical assistance, equipment and building renovations, teacher training, student employment, or whatever that school needs. Such total reliance of a public school on a single private sponsor is a radical alteration of education in America. This conservative trend of market solutions to public problems has an ideological twist when applied to education. The result is not just a better equipped school system. The result is propaganda of commercial values and industrial goals, which runs counter to the democratic principle of education as a free market place of ideas.

Hucksters in America

In 1977, Ralph Nader assigned me to investigate this corporate practice. After three years of survey and evaluation, I documented the extent to which USA corporations promote their products and ideologies to school children. In December 1979, as a final gesture to the International Year of the Child, *Hucksters in the Classroom: A Review of Industry Propaganda in Schools* was published by Nader's Center for Study of Responsive Law in Washington, DC. Though dated, *Hucksters'* evidence endures.

Hucksters' surveys found that 29 per cent of *Fortune* magazine's 500 top industrial corporations, 47 per cent of national trade associations, and 53 per cent of electric-utility companies send *free* teaching materials to the schools. These materials are often specifically tailored for classroom use. They include multiple handouts for students with accompanying teachers' guides. Often the material is graded K-12 and sometimes illustrated with the corporate logo or advertising mascot.

Hucksters cited a teacher's opinion poll by the National Education Association, a USA teachers' union with 1.7 million members. The poll revealed that half of the teachers responding use commercial materials. Such invasions of the classroom are not new. As the first paragraph of *Hucksters* begins:

> Over fifty years ago, Alice Morton now archivist for the National Education Association was in the fifth grade in North Carolina. She remembers her teacher passing out little bars of sweet-smelling green soap supplied by a company representative. Illustrated booklets on the history of soap-making were also distributed. 'I can still smell it now', Ms Morton reminisced. 'And I've been buying Palmolive ever since'. (Harty, 1979)

Case closed. Those who are naive may dismiss the effects of such gratuities or allow their goodwill. But in his 1957 book *The Hidden Persuaders* Vance Packard warned us about the effect of imprint conditioning:

> It takes time, yes, but if you expect to be in business for any length of time, think of what it can mean to your firm in profits if you can condition a million or ten million children who will grow up into adults trained to buy your products as soldiers are trained to advance when they hear the trigger words 'forward march'. (Packard, 1957)

A Captive Audience of Minors

The traditional USA custom has been to use the educational curriculum to promote cultural values and the values of special-interest constituencies. Thus, we have seen curricula innovations for Americanism versus Communism, black studies, women's studies, Third-World studies, environmental education, consumer education, and so forth.

But commercial exploitation of curriculum is qualitatively different and more reprehensible precisely because the sponsors have something to sell. Most schools have bans against solicitation on school grounds. Though the Avon lady can't get in, the high-ranking managers probably could. Material profit is more selfish than ideological propaganda. It distorts the purpose of schools from ideas for enlightenment to ideas for sale. This predominance of commodities, as Ivan Illich writes in *Deschooling Society*, induces a cultural poverty that confines us to survival only through market relations (Illich, 1972).

Sins of omission

In defense, business interests insist that their point of view or special technical knowledge is legitimate subject matter for a relevant curriculum. But consumer education, for example, is more than the exchange of money for a product; it also involves examination of all the prerequisites and consequences of production in a commercial society, including deliberate decision-making and culpable negligence. Such issues critical of businesses' self-interest would not likely be part of their own educational package.

The primary deficiency of commercial materials is their sins of omission that spring from the ideological bias of the sponsoring company's vested interests. For example, *Hucksters* revealed that product information sent to schools by the American Tobacco Institute omits the mention of nicotine and its addictive effects. The presence of caffeine in coffee, cocoa, tea, and cola drinks — and their addictive effects — are also omitted in the information materials sent to schools by the National Coffee Association, the Chocolate Manufacturers Association, the Tea Council, and the National Soft Drink Association.

Such sins of omission are the language of advertising — public relations parading as pedagogy. We should not expect to persuade companies into unrealistic disclosures. But such omissions are evidence of the inherent bias in commercial materials and proof that teachers cannot rely on businesses for accurate or conclusive information. *Hucksters* found that the biggest polluters of the environment — the chemical, steel, and paper industries — were the biggest producers of environmental education material. Their motives seem clear.

Large commercial and industrial firms are trying to distract their critics and win support. Capitalizing on popular consciousness and educational need, business interests have expanded their public-service efforts. Consequently, school children are courted in order to rebuild the corporate image and offset adverse publicity. Indeed, the predominant subjects of commercial materials — energy, environment, nutrition, and economics — are defensive public relations.

Fundraising through brand names

Marketing efforts in the schools go beyond producing instructional materials. Business interests also sponsor contests, field trips, factory tours, and school-assembly programmes. Post Cereals and Campbell Soups sponsor collection drives for box tops and can labels. Thus, neighbourhoods are inundated with underage sales representatives pleading support for their schools through the sale of soup and beans.

Such collection drives usually offer a meagre quid pro quo in audiovisual or athletic equipment to the schools for the required quota of labels collected. The promised bonus to the schools is calculated not on the retail price of the product, however, but on the printing cost of the label! At that rate, it takes thousands of labels just to earn a baseball. Enlightened to this Norway's Fair Trade Regulations prohibit this kind of promotional solicitation to children because it exploits their collection mania.

Cartoons as teachers for kids

Market surveys have shown that children both recall and prefer such corporate cartoon mascots as Kellogg's Tony the Tiger, McDonald's Ronald, and Pillsbury's Dough Boy over their grandpa, daddy, and the local pastor. Knowing this, Exxon commissioned Walt Disney's Mickey Mouse and Goofy to teach about energy to USA school children. The resulting Exxon comic book was distributed free to all members of the National Education Association.

The American Iron and Steel Institute hired Disney's Donald Duck to narrate a film presentation on the history of the US steel industry. Despite the film's denial of the industry's responsibility for pollution and occupational disease and injury, Donald's animated quacking throughout made the film a hit with students.

When corporate curricula efforts succeed as entertainment, they may be suspect as education. Recognizing this vulnerability in children, Great Britain's Code of Advertising Practices prohibits use of familiar cartoon characters because they prey upon a child's natural credulity and sense of loyalty.

Hucksters Around the World

Such corporate activity is by no means confined to the United States or even to industrialized countries. The Third World too is a target for the public-relations expertise of multinationals. The dominance of such giant corporations around the world contributes to a standardized global culture of material gratification. Corporate products also replace native choices for food, drink, clothing, tools, and recreation. These multinationals impinge on the cultural integrity of whole nations, complicating attempts to develop their own resources and values.

The promotion of multinational brand names over local goods is a serious problem for many Third-World nations. Such advertising goes beyond sales and economic effects. It forms attitudes, builds images, and influences behaviour that result in a misappropriation of purchasing power, a loss of native industry, toxicity from unregulated imports, and 'commerciogenic malnutrition' as junkfoods replace local foods.

No global survey exists on the extent to which multinational corporations have invaded cultures around the world through educational disguises. Nor do we have a survey such as *Hucksters* on each country's business involvement in the schools. We do have an industry-sponsored study of seven European countries and a government-sponsored study of four Scandinavian countries.

The Union of Industries of the European Community

UNICE's October 1983 report *Private Industry and Young Consumer Education* provides a survey of national and local business involvement in education from Belgium, France, West Germany, England, Switzerland, the Netherlands, and Ireland. UNICE encourages increased, though responsible, involvement in education by European business interests to bridge the credibility gap between industry and consumers, enhance the deteriorating image of private industry, deflect attacks on products and marketing, and relieve the pressure for government intervention. The report recommends that European firms produce curricula materials, cautions against using the material as propaganda, and praises responsible efforts by businesses to curb abuses.

Many of UNICE's recommendations are laudable: avoidance of advertising, the inclusion of opposition or controversy, the request for teacher feedback, the withdrawal of dated material, the coordination with opposition groups, and the attachment of a nominal cost. Nevertheless, much is omitted. Adequate disclosure of the sponsoring company is needed as primary-source identification on all commercial material. But even such labelling may not enable teachers to evaluate the vested interest bias. Insufficient disclosure of the sponsoring company's product line or investments prohibits a teacher from weighing the material's bias in preparing a balanced lesson plan.

The Secretariat of the Scandinavian Governments

A 1979 report *Advertising in Schools* surveyed teachers' assessment and students' comment on commercial materials in Denmark, Finland, Norway, and Sweden. This report was limited to researching the amount, type, and distribution of commercial materials in elementary schools. The report cites that half to four-fifths of Scandinavian teachers use commercial material. The amount varies between countries (one-third of social studies teachers in Finland; three-fourths in Sweden) and between subjects (80–90 per cent of home economics teachers in all four countries).

Similarities with the *Hucksters'* report are striking. Both reports state that teachers value commercial materials because they are free, different, current, and attractive — and because few alternatives exist. Both reports agree further that:

- Most commercial materials are free, although some audiovisual material incurs costs.
- Most commercial materials are print.
- The subjects covered are predominantly food and nutrition, energy and the environment, and economics.
- Home economics' teachers are the most frequent users of commercial materials.
- The firms that produce the most curricula materials are fuel industries, banks, insurance companies, and food manufacturers.
- The company's name is often not on the materials.
- Availability of commercial materials reaches teachers through educational magazines, teacher-training seminars, educational conferences, and company representatives.

Needed: A Commercial-free Zone

Both the USA and Scandinavian studies reflect the ambivalence of teachers toward the influence of commercial materials on students. Some teachers say that students are not affected because they get commercial messages all the time from television. Other teachers say that students are greatly affected because commercial materials are so attractive. Most teachers, however, say commercial materials are worth using with students if they are used critically with regard to the company's commercial bias.

If teachers recognize the commercial motive of the materials, this presumes a suspicion on the materials' truth or accuracy. What then is the justification for using the materials in a classroom? Such accommodation may be proof of the success of advertising in blunting our critical capacities. Perhaps accommodating underfinanced schools ought to be charging corporations for the advertising time of commercials per student?

Everyone seems to have confidence in the classroom teacher's ability to select materials, assess commercial motives, and counter-balance whatever bias or misinformation exists. Given the complex and technical subjects addressed by business interests, this assurance may be faulty. Most classroom teachers lack the time to review materials before use. Many often lack the expertise to perceive the subtle bias, inaccuracy, or factual omissions as well as to compensate effectively.

Both the USA and Scandinavian studies agree that schools and teachers lend authority and approval to the sponsoring company and to the company's message. Indeed, according to the Scandinavian study, half the teachers using such materials do not even discuss the commercial implications. Without critical evaluation of commercial motives in a discussion between students and teachers, the educational value of commercial materials is surrendered to their promotional intent.

Save the Children

A marketing strategy that seduces children toward brand-name loyalty and corporate myths seems particularly insidious. For children, industry's right to free speech may not even apply. Children are not the assumed rational consumer for whom advertising provides a service of information relevant to logical market behaviour. Such reasoned capacity for free choice is the presupposition of free-speech guarantees. Children, therefore, should be governed by different rules. For a parallel, free-speech rights do not give someone the right to yell 'Fire!' in a crowded auditorium. What about someone yelling 'Ice cream!' in a crowded classroom?

Although commercial speech has usually been an exception to free-speech limitations, captive audiences are also an exception to free-speech guarantees. Thus, market promotion under the guise of educational curricula is especially unconscionable because the classroom constitutes a captive audience of minors. Dr Ed. Goetzmann, a school principal in Bridgewater, New Jersey USA, was inundated with requests to promote products in the schools. His reaction:

> No! Go peddle your wares and humanitarian projects during the 85 per cent of waking hours the children are not in my charge.

Good Fences Make Good Neighbours

Most issues addressed by business interests in their curricula materials deserve public discussion: energy needs and nuclear power, food production and world hunger, industrial technology and toxic-waste disposal. The solutions to these problems involve difficult social, economic, and political choices. And solutions will take time. Consequently, children have become a logical target audience for winning future allies.

Teaching materials are especially valuable for corporation promotion because the context adds value and sanction. Children place trust in those who teach them. Neither consumers nor citizens must surrender this responsibility to business interests. Indeed, children are the vehicles for sustaining social and democratic values.

Sheila Harty

Schools should be an open market place of ideas. They should provide balance and diversity of views and the opportunities for discussion of alternative perspectives. If commercial and industrial interests are in the schools, then consumer and public interests should be there also. When left unchallenged, pervasive corporate influence numbs critical inquiry into the use of economic power in society and dilutes cultural values.

What then are the possible safeguards to curb the excesses or abuses of commercial involvement in education? Both the USA study *Hucksters in the Classroom* and the Scandinavian study *Advertising in Schools* offer similar recommendations for the use of commercial materials in the schools:

- teacher training in critical evaluation of commercial material;
- disclosure labelling of commercial sponsorship;
- recruitment of more alternative materials in counterbalance; and
- more study on the effect of commercial materials on students.

References

DELLABOUGH, R. (1992) *Students Shopping 4 a Better World*, New York, Council on Economic Priorities.

EURICH, N. (1985) *Corporate Classrooms: The Learning Business*, Washington, DC, Carnegie Foundation for the Advancement of Teaching.

HARTY, S. (1979) *Hucksters in the Classroom: A Review of Industry Propaganda in Schools*, Washington, DC, Ralph Nader's Center for Study of Responsive Law.

HARTY, S. (1985) *The Corporate Pied Piper: Ideas for International Consumer Action on Business Propaganda in Schools*, Penang, Malaysia, International Organization of Consumers Unions.

ILLICH, I. (1972) *Deschooling Society*, London, Calder and Boyars.

JACOBSON, M. and MAZUR, L. (in press) *Marketing Madness: What Commercialism is Doing to our Culture*, Boulder, Colorado, Westview Press.

MCNEAL, J. (1992) *Kids as Customers: A Handbook of Marketing to Children*, New York, Free Press, Division of Macmillan Publishing Company.

MOLNAR, A. (in press) *Giving Kids the Business: The Commercialization of American Public Education*, Boulder, Colorado, Westview Press.

PACKARD, V. (1957) *The Hidden Persuaders*, London, Longmans.

SCANDINAVIAN WORKING COMMISSION FOR CONSUMER QUESTIONS (1979) *Advertising in Schools*, Stockholm, Sweden, The Secretariat of the Scandinavian Governments.

UNICE (UNICE CONSUMERS AFFAIRS COMMITTEE) (1983) *Private Industry and Young Consumer Education* (translated from the French), Brussels, Belgium, Union of the Industries of the European Community.

WARD, S. and WARTELLA, E. (1977) *How Children Learn to Buy: The Development of Consumer Information-Processing Skills*, Ann Arbor, Michigan, Books on Demand, University Microfilms International.

Part 2

The Debate in Philosophical and Educational Terms

Chapter 10

Markets, Values and Education

Colin Wringe

Introduction

One of the currently more fashionable doctrines proclaims the practical and, indeed the moral virtues of the so-called free market. Greater use of free-market institutions, it is held, will not only resolve many of our economic problems but also contribute to the well-being of the population at large by allowing to individuals a greater degree of freedom and control over their own lives and developing qualities of independence, self-reliance, intelligence, frankness and self-respect corroded by other modes of arranging our affairs.

It is proposed to refer to these supposed advantages in relation to two contrasting visions of the market place in order to identify certain limitations of the free-market policy and areas of activity to which the appropriateness of market transactions is questionable. In the light of these considerations we shall hopefully be in a position to shed light on the much debated question of whether the provision of education itself may properly be regarded as a marketable commodity.

Two Visions of the Market Place

As regards our first vision of the market place, it is scarcely possible to improve on the idyllic picture provided by Adam Smith in *The Wealth of Nations* (Smith, 1776). Sturdy yeoman and independent artisans bring their surplus produce to exchange in the local town. The uncontrolled rise and fall of prices according to the law of supply and demand ensure that effort and resources are directed to where they are most needed. Besides being economically efficient it is also supposed to be morally pleasing in that producers are encouraged to apply industry, efficiency and ingenuity in the process of production while purchasers become well informed, critical and judicious in their choices. What each has the opportunity to consume is proportionate to what he or she produces and well-being is ensured by the maximization of individual autonomy. The tyranny of occupational direction and controlled consumption is avoided. All appear free to balance their own interests and priorities in choosing how they will fill their working hours and how they will enjoy the fruits of their labour.

Provided it is let alone, the market functions as a well-appointed and self-regulating machine and each individual in seeking his or her own interest is led 'as by an unseen hand' to promote the good of all. In its essential features, this view of the market is retained by the late twentieth-century writers of the New Right (see Graham and Clark, 1986), who emphasize the distortions, inefficiencies and morally corrupting consequences of attempts to interfere with the market mechanism.

Our attitude to the market place must, however, be ambivalent for our second vision, deriving from the nineteenth rather than the eighteenth century and depicted in numberless political tracts, school history books and works of imaginative fiction is altogether less appealing. Here, the locus of production is no longer the rural holding or cottage workshop but the industrial factory. There can be no greater contrast than that between the material and moral conditions of the individuals depicted by our two visions. In the second, Smith's robust and sturdy yeoman artisans are replaced by wage slaves whose squalid conditions and mortal sufferings others have described with vivid realism. Of particular interest, however, is the fact that in this new situation, the institution of free-market exchange has taken on a form which deprives it of its central moral justification.

Essential to Smith's picture of the market place is not equality of wealth but approximate equality of bargaining power. If the wealthy merchants in town will not give us the price for our grain, then be hanged to them. Next year we will lay down roots or grassland for the raising of cattle or, at worst, make a living by cutting faggots at the forest edge. The means of production lie ready to hand. The yeoman has only to supply his energies, will and intelligence. Choice of occupation remains relatively free, as does the management and timing of the working day.

In our second model, the choices of the individual are tightly circumscribed, both as a consumer and, more especially as a producer. Price competition demands mass production and a limited range of products for most people, even if in slightly more affluent times limited variation in products at a superficial and cosmetic level may create an impression of choice. But if the ordinary citizen is offered a limited freedom of choice as a shopper and consumer of entertainments at the weekend, this is more than made up for by the restriction he suffers when he reports for work on Monday morning.

It is a banality of nineteenth and twentieth-century polemics that in a pure market situation the worker is in no position to bargain seriously over the price of his labour for his adversary can afford to wait while he, the worker, must reach agreement urgently or starve. Unlike the yeoman or simple craftsman he cannot turn to the production of other goods, but must take the work offered, for he has access to the means of production only on the proprietor's terms. He is not free to choose the volume, pace or timing of his work, nor will the activity of production develop in him qualities of independence, judgment and intelligence. No unseen hand ensures that *this* market works for the benefit of all, for price competition must constantly force down the market price of labour until, with Malthuisian evolutionary logic, the least viable workers die of malnutrition and disease and scarcity prevents the price of labour from falling further. Smith's self-adjusting, smoothly operating machine is replaced by a mechanism which produces recurrent cycles of slump and boom punctuated by periods of social unrest.

Such justification as existed for this situation was supplied by the infamous Natural Law principle of freedom of contract, according to which any deal was legitimate and binding, however unequal the bargaining positions of those involved when it was struck, (Mabbott, 1947). Modern attempts to alleviate the harshness of freedom of contract in its extreme forms are invariably contentious and much at issue in the contemporary free-market debate. We are therefore led to seek some general principles upon which the action of the free market may be limited and distinctions drawn between those goods and services which are appropriately subject to the market mechanism, and those which are not.

The Limits of Marketability

Smith's prime considerations are that the free market conduces to the good of all, which we must regard as inseparable from the good of the individuals by whom this all is constituted. This good is supposed to be secured in two ways. The free market is assumed to be the arrangement most likely to produce an adequate supply of much needed goods and much desired material prosperity. It also allows individuals to use their resources and efforts to maximize their own advantage by choosing the things they most want for themselves.

In certain circumstances, however, unrestricted operation of the free market or dependence on it is unlikely to prove beneficial:

- Certain activities are inherently detrimental to the public interest or subversive of essential social institutions.
- Market transactions are unsuitable for the distribution of necessities which individuals are unable to meet through no fault of their own, or which are beyond the means of ordinary individuals.
- The same is true for commodities or services to which the principle of *caveat emptor* cannot realistically apply; that is, regarding which individuals are in no position to judge their own needs, or the quality of goods and services supplied, and are thus dependent on the commitment of the supplier rather than their own acumen to safeguard their interests.

Transactions Subversive of Public Institutions

These include transactions based on fraud and deception, agreements that interfere with the working of the market mechanism itself, such as the formation of cartels, monopolies and market corners, the uncontrolled sale of dangerous or harmful items or substances (narcotics, weapons, dangerous toys) and transactions with neighbourhood effects which are grossly disadvantageous to non-beneficiaries (e.g., by despoiling the natural environment).

We no longer countenance the sale of public offices or the giving of back-handers to influence the decisions of officials and politicians, for this is likely to lead to appointments and decisions being made that do less than maximize the public advantage. Market processes also have little part to play in the everyday operation of the law and justice. Police protection would be of little value if it were only available to those able to pay the bill and despite the remark of Brecht's corrupt judge Asdak (Brecht, 1934) that only those should expect justice who can afford to pay for it, venal justice is no justice at all. The continuing practice of treating legal representation as a marketable service in many countries is scarcely legitimate in that it makes the outcome of legal cases partly dependent on the litigant's ability to pay.

Meeting Minimal Needs

An advantage of Smith's model is that all are able to become economically active, and are motivated to do so. In modern reality this may no longer be possible. Without access to organized means of production it may, with the best will in the world, not be possible for an individual to generate the necessary spending power to meet the basic costs of modern life. This situation calls for minimum social-security arrangements, for which two modes of justification may be offered.

The first of these is that such support falls into the category of a welfare right to which we are entitled in return for our obedience to the law and our respect for the rights of others (Wringe, 1981). The second, is that since, by definition such minimal provision applies only when individuals are unable to market their labour for a reasonable return, the only effect of refusing an alternative source of income is to force them into unavoidable poverty or open the way to unequal contracts and labour-market conditions depicted in our second vision and which can in no way be regarded as conducive to the good of all.

There are also certain emergency situations which cannot satisfactorily be met from the resources of ordinary individuals even when they have been reasonably provident. In Smith's vision, producers bring to the market those of their products which are superfluous to their needs and which they exchange for others they need more. This picture is morally acceptable in that the necessities of life can be had in exchange for reasonable quantities of other things which may cost some trouble and expense to put together but can be spared. The things exchanged are of relative value to each other and this value will normally reflect the effort of production as well as the effects of scarcity of abundance.

In the modern world, certain categories of good fall outside these parameters both because their cost at currently acceptable levels of adequacy is disproportionate to the resources of ordinary individuals and because they meet needs that are so extreme that to apply to them relative values in terms of everyday commodities and services would be absurd or morally grotesque. *Pace* Hobbes (Hobbes, 1651), there can be no reasonable basis for bargaining in a life or death situation. Medical care (for serious conditions) may be taken as a paradigm instance of this kind of service. This has not traditionally formed part of the market mechanism for ordinary people. Those who suffered serious accident or illness in the past usually just died, or were cared for by religious or charitable organizations or doctors following the principle of *misericordia non mercede*, who gave their services free.

Areas Where 'Caveat Emptor' Cannot Realistically Apply

A further necessary feature of marketable goods and services — and certainly one present in Smith's simpler vision — is that their quality and value should be assessable by the consumer, for only thus is the producer constrained to give value for money and the act of purchase one of free and rational choice. In our own age of highly complex products, some governments have acted to provide redress for the purchasers of some commodities and services the shortcomings of which only become apparent after purchase. This, however, is not easy to do where the service required or the outcome it is reasonable to achieve cannot be judged by the layman or is difficult to specify in advance.

Those seeking repairs to motor vehicles or electrical appliances may be entirely in the expert's hands in order to know exactly what work needs to be undertaken. More seriously, a medical patient may know he or she wishes to be rid of the pain he or she suffers but be unable to tell whether he or she should seek moderate relief by continuing to take his or her indigestion tablets, or undergo a surgical operation. If the cure is less than entirely satisfactory, should he or she blame the physician and consult someone else next time — if he or she survives and there is a next time — or accept the physician's word that everything has been done that could have been done in his or her case.

Is Education a Marketable Commodity?

McMurtry (1991) draws attention to certain supposed inconsistencies between the values of the market place and the aims of higher education, insofar as research and unfettered enquiry are concerned. Our present concern, however, is with the formal education of younger pupils up to levels compulsory in many advanced countries.

It seems not unreasonable that the purchase of education should be a purely private transaction, like beauty care or driving lessons. Presumably, education is beneficial to its recipients, otherwise it would be unconscionable to oblige children to attend school for eleven or so years as we do at present. If it is beneficial, then is it not reasonable that those who benefit should pay? Those who thought it was not beneficial or preferred to put their time and resources to other use would then be free to do so. Something similar was proposed by Illich (1971) and the deschoolers in the 1970s.

In a free-market situation different teachers or educational firms would offer education of different kinds, qualities and durations. This might be in the form of a complete educational package analogous to our present full-time education, or it might be a partial service in say, writing, arithmetic, technology or Bible study. Customers would choose what they wanted, and expect to get what they paid for. Those who didn't think they were getting their money's worth would take their custom elsewhere. Teachers would have an interest in being considerate, conscientious and pedagogically skilled, on pain of finding themselves out of business. There is a slight complication in the fact that the consumer, the child, is not the same person as the purchaser, the parent, but is this so very different from the situation in which the parent buys the child a winter coat? This may occasionally result in the child not getting the coat he or she has set his or her heart on, but does not seriously undermine the market process.

Beauty care, driving lessons and winter coats are fairly typical marketable goods and services. The purpose of what follows is to argue, that by its nature, education does not fall into this category.

Treating Education as a Marketable Commodity Would Be Inherently Detrimental

My first two arguments for taking education out of the market mechanism and the realm of individual choice are embarrassing to the liberal mind in that they involve coercing the individual child for the greater good or convenience of the adult community. Happily, however, arguments have been produced for believing that compulsory education of the right kind will increase rather than restrict the autonomy of the individual (White, 1973).

The adult community needs to subject children to custodial constraint during the daytime when parents are otherwise occupied. Failure to do so, besides being troublesome to the adult community, would expose the young to both physical and moral danger. To simply incarcerate children for some eleven years, however, would be unacceptable and requires some substantial compensation in terms of the benefit the children receive in consequence. It is difficult to think of any purpose other than education to which this time might be put with such good justification. Eleven years of compulsory entertainment and amusement would not be an acceptable alternative.

The community as a whole also has an interest in the education of its members. The prosperity of individuals depends not only on their own skills and resources but also on those of the community around them. Though the potential of education for social control may sometimes be a temptation to unscrupulous governments it also has positive value as an instrument of government, delivering a literate population and establishing civilized norms upon which society depends for both humane social management and rational change.

But not only would market choice of having or not having education be detrimental to the good of all. There are also grave objections to a situation in which all receive education of a sort but different varieties and qualities of education are available according to the customer's choice and pocket. If education were to form a fairly substantial family investment in competition with other important goods such as housing, holidays, transport or the needs of the family business, even caring parents would feel obliged to seek a form of education stressing opportunities either for narrowly vocational skill learnings or social advancement. The education of all children may legitimately contain elements of these but it seems likely that in an educational market situation only extremely wealthy parents who had themselves received a generously conceived liberal education would feel able to provide the kind of education aimed at all-around development of the child and initiation into non-utilitarian activities and goals.

One hesitates to suggest that parents are less capable of choosing in the long-term interests of their children than educationalists or governments. However, it is nevertheless a feature of education that its full value can only be appreciated after it has been received, and of the modern world that in the foreseeable future each generation is likely to receive a more developed and sophisticated education than its parents. Where, as in the UK, attempts have been made to give parents greater control over their children's education, this has been part of a political campaign to favour more traditional, authoritarian teaching methods, concentration on the so-called basics of the curriculum and the avoidance of critical or radical curriculum content. The expectation is that parents will prefer a form of education similar to that they themselves received as children, in an earlier and more illiberal age.

A community's culture as mediated via its education system must be largely common to all citizens if that community is not to disintegrate. Certain assumptions, undertstandings, pieces of knowledge and educational opportunities need to be offered to all citizens if the society is not simply to become a rag-bag of separate and possibly hostile groups occupying the same territory. The supposed right of parents to ensure that their children are brought up according to their own religious or philosophical beliefs needs to be balanced not only against the public interest but also the rights of children not to be excluded from the mainstream culture of their society (Cohen, 1981).

If different qualities of education are offered at different prices this will promote social stratification. The extent to which this is acceptable will naturally depend on one's larger political commitments. The development of a large underclass of semi-socialized semi-literates produced by the lowest quality of education, offered at the lowest price must, however, be alarming to all. Any arrangement that results in the systematic segregation of children from different backgrounds must have the effect of perpetuating social and educational disadvantage. If higher-quality education is the gateway to higher-status occupations — and this is certainly believed by many who pay for their children's education in Anglo-Saxon countries — then the purchase of higher-quality education for one's children is equivalent to the purchase of public offices.

This particular defect of a free market in education remains present and may even be exacerbated in certain educational mixed economies that either exist or have been proposed. These include Mill's proposal (Mill, 1867) of laying down minimum educational requirements while leaving individual parents to ensure that this minimum is met and provide more if they wish, making minimum educational provision for all children in state institutions, allowing or encouraging superior or reputedly superior private institutions to flourish alongside them, offering vouchers for the price of minimum educational provision to the parents of all children and allowing wealthier parents to top these with an additional payment to secure education of a higher quality (Friedman, 1962).

Education Is Something We Cannot Do Without

If the market mechanism is used for goods and services we cannot do without, this may result in some people being deprived of things that are welfare rights, and there is no point in making the purchase of something a subject of choice when there is no way we can choose to do without it. We may think that some children, especially some adolescents, may only too readily choose to do without education but this misconstrues the notion of choosing, which, in its full sense, entails an awareness of the implications of one's choice. It is a justification of the free market that individuals are able to choose how they will expend their resources, but not if they do not get what they think they are getting (or lose something they do not know they are losing) when they make one choice rather than another.

In arguing elsewhere that education is a welfare right (Wringe, 1986) I have drawn attention to the appalling situation of someone deprived of basic socialization into the various forms of human knowledge and understanding. Even if we limit use of the term 'education' to that which is received at school, however, individuals without education in even this sense may find themselves in an unenviable situation in a market polity, in the modern world, not merely in a very weak bargaining position in the labour market but unable to enter it at all, and thus denied the human right of participation in the cultural life and practical activities of their community.

Quite apart from material considerations the person without education, or whose education is inadequate suffers losses in quality of life, a range and richness of experience and personal autonomy which no one would willingly choose in full knowledge of what was involved. Like medical treatment, however, the full cost of adequate provision is disproportionate to the resources of ordinary people and, again like medical care, has traditionally been taken out of the mainstream market mechanism, if not by the State, then by religious or other charitable organizations. Even many of the most prestigious, supposedly private schools, in which parents nowadays pay a major part of the cost of the education received, are not strictly market organizations run for profit and aiming primarily to serve customer preference, but trusts or similar bodies set up for the purpose of promoting certain educational or other ideals.

The Customer Is Not Well Placed to Judge the Value and Quality of Education

Where the customer is unable to assess the value and quality of the product, two important arguments in favour of the market mechanism are invalidated: the discipline on the producer to strive for excellence and the maximization of the benefit to the consumer who is normally supposed to be the best judge of his own interest. In the case of technical appliances and medical treatment considered above the consumer's inability to choose is purely contingent. People just do not happen to know enough, but in principle they might do so.

In the case of education there is arguably a more fundamental problem. Writers such as Flew (1976) and Olafson (1973) have drawn attention to the asymmetrical nature of the teacher–pupil relationship. It is supposedly inherent in this relationship that one partner knows something that the other does not. To an extent the argument, as presented by both writers, is overstated, even hysterical. Teaching and learning are often cooperative activities in which both parties have a positive contribution to make and learners may often have a clear notion of what it is they want to learn, even if the detailed content is as yet unfamiliar.

At some stage in all areas of study, however, the pupil is necessarily dependent on the teacher's view of what counts as adequate performance. More importantly, pupils will often be dependent on the teacher's understanding of the point of many educational activities and, indeed, the point of the educational process as a whole. There is more to mathematics than getting one's sums right by whatever process seems to deliver the right answer. Historical understanding is more about drawing reasonable inferences from evidence than simply stating correctly what is supposed to have happened and education in science is as much about respect for truth and evidence as about memorizing useful formulae. Yet none of these things may be obvious, even to relatively successful pupils left to their own devices. Teacher who dictate a good set of notes and insist you learn your facts and formulae may well be thought superior to those who ask a lot of apparently pointless questions and do not seem too sure of the answers themselves.

The educational aim of developing interests that the pupil does not already have is at variance with the good marketing principle of following consumer choice, especially if the early stages of learning a particular subject are tedious or difficult. There is also a contradiction in the notion of potential learners choosing an education that will make them more moral (e.g., less self-interested) or less certain of their prejudices and assumptions. Yet precisely these are the achievements of high-quality education. Educators may practise the traditional educational conspiracy of attacting learners by the prospect of material advancement in the hope that they will be seduced into a commitment to study for its own sake (Peters, 1966). But far from being a vindication of the market principle, this would depend precisely on consumers not understanding what their choices are likely to let them in for.

It is true that, as mentioned earlier, the purchasers, as opposed to the consumers, of education are normally parents rather than children. In principle many of these might well see the point of history or science, and be glad to see their enthusiasms being passed on to their children. They might even be glad to see their children being taught the values of altruism and self-doubt, understanding with Plato that true well-being consists as much in moral and intellectual excellence as in material advantage. Some indeed might be as well educated as the educators themselves, or better. In the real world, however, this will not universally be the case and the parents of many children will be bound to depend on such meretricious criteria as a school's social standing, examination results, or the resemblance of its curriculum to the traditional brand of education they themselves received. Teachers and schools already find it difficult enough to enlist the support of parents for liberal and enlightened educational aims. How much more difficult would such a task be in the face of contradiction not motivated by genuine or sincere dissent but forming part of the promotional material of rival institutions aimed at potential customers' baser instincts and insecurities, for such is the character of promotional material in the modern market place. If education were to become a market commodity in the present situation of relative educational ignorance on the part of the general public, this situation would be self-perpetuating, for parents would be bound to choose schools which would pass on their own limited values and understandings to their children, as indeed does happen when parents purchase private education. Educational anti-marketeers are therefore entitled to argue that the marketization of education must wait until the ideal situation is reached in which the admittedly contingent inability of parents to make valid educational choices for their children has been overcome.

In this connection it may be helpful to distinguish between two different conceptions of education which, for convenience, may be labelled the 'service' and the 'vanguard' conceptions. According to the service conception, the adult community has a perfectly satisfactory set of values, understanding and knowledge and simply employs a staff of pedagogues to instill these into the next generation. For teachers to criticize or presume to offer something better would be sheer impertinence. They are simply to teach what they are paid to teach, and that is all.

According to the vanguard conception, the academic/educational/cultural/ world is constantly and necessarily engaged in criticism and speculation and therefore permanently out of step with the majority of adults whose own education may have been perfectly satisfactory at the time but whose last contact with education may have been twenty, thirty or fifty years ago. According to the service conception it is perfectly possible for some parents to know and choose the kind of education for their children and identify the institution most likely to provide it. On the vanguard conception each generation is necessarily unable to judge the educational offerings available to the next. The vanguard conception, however, contains the alarmingly elitist assumption that cultural advance is the prerogative of people in educational and cultural institutions and that others simply wait for news of their progress to trickle down to them. It also makes the arrogant assumption that what is thought to be cultural advance in such places invariably is so, rather than some fashionable aberration, rightly recognized as such by the population at large.

Against this, the service conception is unrealistic in that it is impossible to imagine individuals who are daily concerned with knowledge and ideas but are not disposed to criticize and reflect upon them. Nor is it possible, without criticism and reflection, to engage in such fundamental educational activities as e.g., science, history, social enquiry or aesthetic and moral judgment, or convey the spirit of these activities to the young.

It is this concern with speculation and criticism which ultimately renders true education unmarketizable. It empowers individuals to make choices that are unintelligible to them before the process has taken place, so we cannot meaningfully choose our own education and its outcomes. But equally, being subversive of authority, it liberates the recipient from those who provide it. For given its emphasis on criticism and reflection, we cannot stipulate its outcomes in advance. It cannot therefore coherently be purchased for others by the economic rational man seeking to maximize his own advantage. In mockery of all market principles, therefore, it can only be freely and generously given, or viewed as a right belonging equally to citizens of the next and all succeeding generations, irrespective of the ability to pay.

References

BRECHT, B. (1934) *Der Kaukasische Kreidekreis*, in W. HECHT (Ed) (1985), Frankfurtam-Main, Suhrkamp, p. 80.

Cohen, B. (1981) *Education and the Individual*, London, Allen and Unwin, pp. 25–35.

Flew, A.G.N. (1976) *Sociology Equality and Education*, London, Macmillan, pp. 79–97.

Friedman, M. (1962) *Capitalism and Freedom*, Chicago, Chicago University Press.

Graham, D. and Clarke, P. (1986) *The New Enlightenment*, London, Macmillan.

Hobbes, T. (1651) *Leviathan*, in Macpherson, C.B. (Ed) (1968), Harmondsworth, Penguin, Pt. 4, Ch. 14, p. 198.

Illich, I.D. (1971) *Deschooling Society*, London, Calder and Boyars.

Mabbott, J.D. (1947) *The State and the Citizen*, London, Hutchinson, pp. 62–3.

McMurtry, J. (1991) 'Education and the market model', *Journal of Philosophy of Education*, 25, 2, pp. 209–18.

Mill, J.S. (1867) 'Inaugural address at the University of St. Andrews', quoted in Garforth, F.W. (1979), *John Stuart Mill's Theory of Education*, Oxford, Martin Robertson.

Olafson, F.A. (1973) 'Rights and duties in education' in Doyle, J.F. *Educational Judgments*, London, Routledge and Kegan Paul, pp. 173–95.

Peters, R.S. (1966) *Ethics and Education*, London, Allen and Unwin, pp. 43–5.

Plato, *The Republic*, translation Lee, H.D.P. (1956), Harmondsworth, Penguin, Pt. 1, Bk. 2, pp. 87–99.

Smith, A. (1776) *An Inquiry into the Nature and Causes of the Wealth of Nations*, in Campbell, R.H. and Skinner, A.S. (1976), Oxford, Oxford University Press, pp. 73–4.

White, J.P. (1973) *Towards a Compulsory Curriculum*, London, Routledge and Kegan Paul, pp. 23–5.

Wringe, C.A. (1981) *Children's Rights*, London, Routledge and Kegan Paul, pp. 81–2.

Wringe, C.A. (1986) 'The Human right to education', *Educational Philosophy and Theory*, 18, 2, pp. 31–41.

Chapter 11

Education and the Limits of the Market

John White

Introduction

Chubb and Moe (1990) claim that US public schools are by and large inefficient, that is, are failing in their core academic mission. This is because they are hampered by bureaucracy arising out of democratic procedures of organization and control. This is especially true of inner-city schools. It would be better if parents were given the freedom to choose which schools they wanted to send their children to. Any group or organization can set up a public school as long as it meets minimum state criteria. Such schools would have considerable powers to determine their own curriculum and form of government. A voucher system giving greater benefits to poorer parents could help to ensure an equitable system.

In my contribution I shall not tangle with the empirical claims about the alleged failure of American schools and its causes but concentrate on the recommendation that it is best to move to an (internal) market as outlined. In what I say I shall have in mind the relevance this may have to education in England and Wales.

Chubb and Moe and the Diminution of the Power of the State

In considering what should be the proper limits of the State's responsibilities in the area of schooling, we should distinguish between: its powers to determine school aims and curricula; its powers to own and organize schools; and its powers to direct pupils to specific schools. In England and Wales the State has at present extensive powers in both the first two areas: there is a National Curriculum; and most schools belong to the State, including its local authorities. (Voluntary-aided schools are financed by the State, but have their own governing bodies.) As for the power to direct children to specific schools, state bodies have this to some extent only. For many years parents have been able to express preferences about which state schools should take their children; and local authorities have to take these preferences into account in making their allocations of pupils to schools. Recent legislation has provided parents with greater information about the performance of individual schools to help them in their statements of preference. In the USA, as I understand it, state power over public schools is more extensive, given that 'state power' in this context refers largely to the powers of individual states and of their local organs, especially neighbourhood school boards. The State lays down aims and curricula, owns all the public schools and directs where children should study without allowing parents any say in the matter: everything is decided by the neighbourhood catchment area.

It is clear that Chubb and Moe would like to see a diminution of state power in all three areas. How far in each of them would they want to go?

- Among the minimal state criteria which all schools would have to follow in their alternative system are 'graduation requirements' (Chubb and Moe, 1990, p. 219). They do not say what these should be, beyond the statement that they should roughly correspond to criteria used by many American states in accrediting private schools. They do not, then, believe that the State should have no role in determining a school's aims and curricula. But they do not discuss the principles by which the proper extent of state involvement should be determined. In general, however, they see schools themselves as making the major curriculum decisions. Power here thus shifts from the State to the schools themselves. In effect, though, curricular power passes to the parents, given their role in choosing schools: parents preferring a curriculum based on elements a,b,c rather than d,e,f can choose a school based on the former pattern.
- As I understand things, the State will no longer own any public school. Non-state bodies and organizations alone, including existing private schools, will be able to set up/be redefined as public schools.
- The State will also lose all its powers to allocate children to specific schools. The market system will mean that parents are maximally free to send their children where they wish. If they are unlucky in meeting their preferences, they will not be obliged by the State to send their children to this or that school, but will presumably have to make do with whatever they can still manage to get in the marketplace.

Chubb and Moe do not themselves go into a principled defence of these claims. How far are they in fact defensible?

Who Should Determine a School's Aims and Curriculum?

I have argued elsewhere (White, 1990, Ch. 1) that in a democratic society the broad framework of aims and curricula should be laid down by the State. The reasoning goes like this. Decisions about this broad framework — given minimal conditions of rationality — are decisions about the kind of society one would like to see come into being or continue in existence. Such decisions are political decisions. Decisions about aims and curricula are in this regard on all fours with decisions about taxation policy or national defence. On political policies like these latter two, we hold that every citizen should be entitled to an equal voice. This follows from the principle of political equality written into our generally accepted understanding of democracy. Hence power is put into the hands of an elected government. To leave a section of the population to decide would offend against democratic principles. The same points follow through for decisions about aims and curricula. Here, too, every citizen should have an equal voice; and sectional decision-making should be ruled out. Parents, like teachers, constitute a section of the population merely. To leave wide curricular powers in the hands of parents would offend against the requirement of political equality.

This is not to say that parents should have no curricular powers. There is a good reason why, while the main framework of a school's aims and curricula should be laid down by the State, as one proceeds into details more and more decision-making powers should be allowed to educators: they are in the best position, in principle, to know what routes to politically decided objectives are likely to be best for particular pupils, given what they know about the subject-matter they are teaching, pupils' abilities and needs, as well as a whole host of other local circumstances. At school level, the 'educators' in question are in the first place the school's teachers. But if one accepts the principle that teachers should work in partnership with parents, on the grounds that both parties are to be seen as educators, it is likely that, where appropriate, parents could sometimes collaborate in (relatively minor) curricular decisions.

How far do the Chubb and Moe proposals conform to the principles put forward in the last two paragraphs? The fact that they require minimum graduation requirements on schools seems to imply that they accept some version of the principle that the broad framework of aims and content should be laid down by a democratically elected government. At the same time, they clearly want parents to be given much greater curricular powers. It looks, therefore, as if their proposals are not wholly in line with the principles, although it is hard to tell, short of a more detailed account than they give of which bodies — state, schools, parents — should have which powers.

I have argued that parents should have at most relatively minor curricular powers. Is there anything to be said on the other side? Implicit in the Chubb and Moe view is — given the qualifications in the last paragraph — that in a market-led education system, the consumer rather than the State is to decide what kind of education there should be for a particular child, the consumer being the parent.

Why should the parent be seen as the consumer rather than the child? There is a slight danger of ambiguity here. In a weaker sense the consumers of school education are the pupils themselves: they are the ones who are acquiring knowledge, skills etc. But 'consumer' in the context of a market system implies more than acquiring goods: in its strongest sense it also implies being in the most appropriate position to make choices about which goods to acquire. Let me fill out this idea somewhat. In a market system individuals choose goods according to their preferences and goods are produced to meet those preferences. The individuals themselves are the authorities on what their preferences are. That is why decisions about which socks or fruit to buy (and this has implications for production) are most appropriately made not by the State, but by the individual.

This is what may be called the 'ideal' concept of the consumer in market theory. In practice consumers of groceries, motor cars etc. may not be in the most appropriate position to make choices about these things: hence demands for 'consumer education', the publication *Which?*, and so on. We may call consumers in this sense 'empirical consumers'. But the notion of the empirical consumer within market theory depends on the notion of the ideal consumer. Market theory starts from the idea that the most appropriate persons to make decisions about what goods are to be bought — and therefore produced — are those who acquire the goods. In practice, the latter may need further information or skills to bring them closer to the position of the ideal consumer.

Pupils are consumers of education in the weaker sense — i.e., acquirers of dispositions, knowledge etc. But they are by and large not in a position to choose what they should study or why they should study it: they are insufficiently knowledgeable about such matters. They are not consumers in the stronger, market sense of ideal consumer, since they are not in the most appropriate position to make decisions about what to acquire. Neither can they be seen as empirical consumers, as imperfect approximations to this ideal: their deficiency here cannot be remedied by a quick injection of information, paralleling an inspection of *Which?*; or by a lengthier induction into everything needed to decide on their curriculum, since this would — at the very least — require them virtually to complete their education before they could decide what it should consist in. All this leads back to the thought that the consumers in the stronger sense must be parents. Although they are not themselves acquirers of knowledge, dispositions etc., cannot they be seen as proxy-consumers, acting on behalf of their children in choosing schools with such and such aims and curricula?

A useful comparison here might be with the parents' role in buying food or clothing for their very young children, say infants. Here again the children are the consumers in the weaker sense that they actually eat the food and wear the clothes. But it is the parents who buy these things and (let us suppose) make the decisions. Part of their role as parents is to have some hand in shaping the food-, clothing-, and other preferences of their infant children. Until the children come to have settled and sensible preferences of their own, it is the parents' preferences on their behalf which count. It is thus the parents who are the consumers in the stronger sense. Can we make the same moves, *mutatis mutandis*, for education?

Implicit in this account is the assumption that parents are in the most appropriate position to decide what their children should eat or wear — or, at least, that the parents could easily acquire the relevant information to be in this position. While this may be thought acceptable enough for infants, it may seem less so as children grow older and form their own food and clothing preferences. Here parents may still be consumers in that they buy the goods, but decisions as to what to buy may be to a large extent the children's. This brings in a second sense of 'proxy-consumer', one in which, unlike the sense we have been discussing, the roles of buyer and decider are separated. But for present purposes, i.e., in trying to identify the consumer in the educational context, we can ignore this second sense, given that children are not in a position to decide aims and curricula. The relevant comparison is between the parent as decision-maker and purchaser of food and clothes for infants and the parent as chooser of a school with such-and-such aims and curricula. Can the latter, like the former, be a proxy-consumer in the first sense?

If the answer is 'yes', then parents must be in the most appropriate position to decide what their children should be studying and why. But what grounds are there for this? Can it be that only parents — and not the State or other bodies — have the relevant knowledge for making such decisions? If so, how would this be shown? Parents do indeed sometimes think they know such things, but beliefs, as always, may be false. Just because a devout parent thinks that his or her son should be brought up as a devout Catholic, Seventh Day Adventist, Moslem or whatever, it does not follow that he or she is right.

Parents may reply that they have an obligation as Catholics (etc.) to bring their child up in their faith: this means leaving it to the religious authorities to decide what kinds of aims and curricula are best. This would shift the grounds for the parents' right to decide from unique knowledge to prior commitment. But how strong is this argument? Law — whether secular or religious — does not always coincide with morality or what is ethically desirable. If one is legally obliged to do x, it does not follow that x is what one should do from a moral or ethical point of view. If the religious law in operation in a state says that anyone caught swearing should receive a hundred lashes, it does not follow that this is, from an ethical point of view, what should happen. Similarly, if parents are obliged by some religious law to keep their child from all contact with the theory of evolution, it does not follow that this is ethically what they should do.

More could be said about these and other suggested grounds for the claim that parents are in the most appropriate position to decide about aims and curricula as well as food and clothes. But a powerful argument against this claim has already been mentioned: that every citizen in a liberal democracy, and not only parents, should have an equal say in determining schools' aims and curricula. This argument needs to go one stage deeper. There must be constraints on what this 'equal say' should be. It would be contrary to the democratic ideal if it allowed a majority to elect a government committed to an anti-democratic national curriculum. There are constraints on permissible nationally-determined aims and curricula arising from democratic values themselves: if a democratic society is to continue, strengthened, into the future, schools must bring up pupils to live according to these values. This argument needs further elaboration, but it strongly suggests that to identify consumers in the context of aims and curricula with parents is deeply problematic.

If children are not consumers, and parents are not consumers, who are? If, as I believe, the only persons who can legitimately decide on aims and curricula are citizens (and then only within constraints), then shall we say that the consumer is the citizen? This would be very odd. If citizens decide, then the State in some form decides. But if the State decides, it is not the market that decides. Since the concept of consumer is tied to the concept of market and state provision excludes market provision, citizens cannot be consumers.

We are dealing with two fundamentally different kinds of decision-making, each with its own legitimate rationale. In a market system it is individuals who decide what goods to buy to promote their own flourishing according to their own preferences — an area where only they can make authoritative decisions. In civic decision-making individuals make decisions not about their own flourishing but about the flourishing of a whole community and it is their collective preference, as expressed through democratic procedures, which is authoritative. The proper conclusion is that there is no room for the concept of consumer in decisions about aims and curricula. The consumer is not merely a decider, but a decider within a market. If the market is ruled out, there can still be deciders — i.e., citizens — but no longer room for consumers.

Who Should Own Schools?

We turn now to Chubb and Moe's claim that ideally the State should no longer own public schools. On this issue I am agnostic, conceding that they may have a case. Non-state bodies may often be committed to owning and running schools of high quality. In principle every child might be attending such a school. I can see no reason of principle why the State must own and run its own schools. In this respect, the second issue is importantly different from the first issue (see 'Chubb and Moe and the Diminution of the Power of the State' above).

The crucial thing, it seems to me, is not who owns a school, but whether the school conforms to certain criteria of adequacy — as regards health and safety, for instance, but also as regards aims and curricula. It is up to the State to formulate and enforce such criteria. Chubb and Moe appear to agree in principle with this, although I may find myself disagreeing with them about what the criteria should be. This is likely in the sphere of aims and curricula, as we have seen. It may also pertain in the sphere of school organization. Chubb and Moe state that 'each school must be granted sole authority to determine its governing structure. It may be entirely run by teachers or even the unions. It may vest all its power in a principal' (Chubb and Moe, 1990, p. 223). It seems to me that whether there should be more stringent state criteria about school organization depends, among other things, on interrelationships between school organization on the one hand and aims and curricula on the other. Suppose, for instance, that among state criteria to do with aims and curricula is the requirement that schools prepare pupils for their responsibilities as democratic citizens. (For reasons spelt out elsewhere, I would indeed, include that among the criteria). If a school is allowed — as in the Chubb and Moe scheme, it seems — to be run on authoritarian lines, that may hinder rather than encourage in pupils the cultivation of democratic dispositions. In which case there may have to be state criteria charging every school to be run more democratically. (Again, I personally would want to argue for this.)

I have conceded that in principle there may be a case, as yet unexamined, for non-state bodies to own and run the public schools. In practice, however, there could well be difficulties in leaving everything to voluntary provision. What if there were not enough non-state schools to go round, since not enough potential owners came forward? At the very least, the State has a duty to ensure that all children have a school to go to; and, if voluntary provision is insufficient, the State may have to have schools of its own. There are also practical problems given that nearly all schools are as things are state-owned and run. To what extent a shift towards voluntary provision should be encouraged depends on whether it is on balance harmful for particular schools to be owned by the State. Very many state schools are excellent institutions. I see no reason of principle why they should be replaced by non-state schools.

Who Should Decide Which Schools Children Attend?

The third issue is whether the State should have powers to direct children to specific schools or whether parents should be maximally free to pick which schools they wanted. Here I find myself torn on what is, after all, a matter more of practical politics than of philosophical argument. (See on this Morris's contribution to this volume.) On the one hand, one hears stories of countries like Finland, for instance, where children automatically go to neighbourhood schools with no choice of schools possible, and where the system seems to work well and creates no pressure for change. (But how far is the Finnish experience premised on widespread affluence and social/cultural homogeneity?)

On the other hand, there also seem to be good reasons in a society like

Britain or the USA why parents should have some say over choice of schools. If they have no say, they may be stuck with a school which is unsuitable in some way: it might be too hard or dangerous for their child to get to; its ethos and teaching arrangements may not suit their child's temperament or range of abilities. Parents, as partners in the educational enterprise, have the responsibility to see that their child attends a school where he or she can flourish and learn productively. Without being privileged experts on the best aims and curricula for schools in general, they are often privileged experts when it comes down to their own child's specific circumstances and characteristics. So there is something of a case — not necessarily an overriding case — for parental choice of schools — a case which has long been acknowledged in the British system if not in the American. In principle it would be a good thing if all parents could place their children in schools with which they felt comfortable, provided as always that every school conformed to state criteria of different sorts.

In practice, once again, there would be difficulties in realizing this ideal. Not every parent would be likely to get their first choice of school and some mechanisms would have to be found to minimize unfairnesses arising from the efforts of more thrusting parents — usually those higher up the socio-economic scale — to get their children into schools with the best teachers or the best track-record in maximizing their life-chances. The kind of voucher system that Chubb and Moe put forward, which is weighted towards the most disadvantaged families, is one such mechanism and is worth exploring further. (See also on this Naismith's contribution to this volume.)

One last, important, point. In Chubb and Moe's scheme, as in the present British government's, parents should have greater powers in choosing schools in virtue of their role as consumers. As I argued earlier, however, the concept of consumer does not apply to parents. There are no good reasons for claiming that they are in the most appropriate position to judge what kind of education is best for their children to have (even though they may sometimes be in a good position to say that one school is more likely to be beneficial than another). If parents are to have powers to influence the placing of their children, this is not because they are consumers and this brings with it certain rights, but because (see Bridges' contribution to this volume) they are educators and this brings with it certain responsibilities.

Acknowledgment

I would like to thank Patricia White for her help in encouraging me to focus in this chapter on the concept of the consumer; and Steve Bramall for his comments on an earlier draft which led me to what I hope is greater precision on the matter of consumers' being in the most appropriate position to make decisions. An earlier version of this chapter was presented in a symposium on 'Education, the market and the state: perspectives from Great Britain' to the Annual Meeting of the US Philosophy of Education Society at New Orleans in March 1993.

References

CHUBB, J.E. and MOE, T.M. (1990) *Politics, Markets and America's Schools*, Washington DC, The Brookings Institute.

WHITE, J.P. (1990) *Education and the Good Life: Beyond the National Curriculum*, London, Kogan Page.

Chapter 12

Education is a Public Good:
On the Need to Resist the
Domination of Economic Science

Gerald Grace

Introduction

Education and the Market Place, the title of this book, encapsulates a major
cultural and ideological debate which has taken place throughout the 1980s
and which remains central to public discussion about education in the 1990s.
At the heart of this debate are major differences about the nature and purpose
of public education and about the most desirable and effective means of providing it as a service to the community. For some contributions to this debate,
see Tomlinson (1986), The Hillgate Group (1987), Dale (1989), Ball (1990),
Cultural Studies, Education Group (1991), Green (1991), Simon (1992).

If this debate is set in an historical context it can be seen that, in a number
of societies, an established social democratic consensus about the nature of
education has been radically challenged by New-Right arguments deriving,
among other things, from versions of free-market economics. The social
democratic consensus, in England and New Zealand for instance, has been
that education is a public good and an essential service to all citizens which
should be provided by the State universally, without direct charge and with
an aspiration to provide equal educational opportunities. The New-Right
challenge of the 1980s has been to argue that education is not a public good
but a commodity in the market place and that this commodity would be
delivered more efficiently and effectively to its consumers (parents and children) if the State progressively withdrew its involvement, leaving the 'hidden
hand' of market forces to provide the optimum solution to issues of both
effectiveness and of equality of opportunity. These are matters of such fundamental importance for the shaping of public policy that it is essential that this
debate should involve as many citizens in a given society as possible. The
issues are far too important to be left to politicians, ideologues, educationalists, economists and philosophers.

The key constituency for the resolution of these issues must be that of a confident and well-informed democratic community. It is one of the arguments of this chapter that the exponents of particular forms of technical expertise have attempted during the 1980s to capture positions of dominance in public discourse. The strategy of these technical (and ideological) positions has been to suggest that 'in the real world' (which they construct) certain powerful concepts and laws operate which have to be accepted in modern, forward-looking societies. In the realm of the social sciences such claims can be made by a variety of experts representing a range of academic disciplines. The charge is frequently made by certain political and ideological interest groups that sociologists and educationalists achieved far too much prominence in the public discourse of the 1960s and 1970s. Part of the current reaction to this claimed dominance is a contemporary appeal either to 'common sense' or to the 'economics of the real world'. In the 1980s it can be seen that such claims have been made most confidently (and some would say most arrogantly) by protagonists of particular versions of economic science. The subtitle of this chapter, 'On the Need to Resist the Domination of Economic Science' gives the prime focus for my argument. Economists, and those using the discourse of economics, are entitled to make a case that education is a commodity in the market place and not, as was previously supposed, a public good. They are, of course, entitled to argue that the operation of the disciplines of the market place will enhance the quality of the educational services available to all citizens. What they are not entitled to do is to try to make themselves the popes of the modern age, whose doctrines, faith and *ex cathedra* pronouncements have to be taken as definitive within any sector of public-policy debate. It should be said here, in fairness, that these Roman pretensions are held by only a sector of those practising economic science. Nevertheless those holding such views tend to be strategically placed in advisory positions to various governments at this time, as will be demonstrated later.

This chapter will make a case that education is a public good and that, this being so, it should be provided primarily by the State and without direct charge, to all citizens. The phrase 'primarily by the State' is taken to imply educational provision by democratically elected central and local governments, supplemented by free provision from religious or voluntary agencies. The phrase 'without direct charge' recognizes that the costs of education are considerable but argues that these should be met through the public-taxation system and not directly by the user. This case is made as a contribution to contemporary public debate. It is taken as axiomatic in this strategic area of public policy that an informed democratic community will evaluate the strengths and weaknesses of this argument in relation to various counter arguments and alternative theses on this subject. In keeping with the view that matters of this sort should be located in historical and socio-cultural contexts, the structure of this chapter will outline the writer's own involvements in education-market place debates in both New Zealand and England. An attempt will then be made to construct a more developed position on education as as public good, arising from these earlier papers and exchanges.[1]

Gerald Grace

Economic Science and Education: Arguments Visible and Invisible

In 1987, the economists of the New Zealand Treasury produced a major document on education policy for the advice of the in-coming Labour government of Mr David Lange, (New Zealand Treasury, 1987). This Treasury Brief (of 295 pages!) was clearly designed to have a formative influence on public discussion of education issues in New Zealand and on the shaping of future education policy. It has since its publication been at the centre of education-market place debates in New Zealand, (see Middleton *et al.*, 1990, and Manson, 1992 for a review of sources). However this document has a significance which extends well beyond the cultural, economic and political context of New Zealand. What it does, in an unprecedented way, is to make quite explicit and visible the arguments, assumptions and strategies employed by certain market economists when they review education. In other contexts of public and official discussion about education, the incremental commodification of education has taken place at a more implicit and invisible level, generally beginning with a process of language change in which curricula are 'delivered', parents become 'consumers', and schools are assessed on 'output' characteristics. In other words, the commodification of education is implied but not explicitly stated. The New Zealand Treasury brief has the virtue of bringing to the surface and making quite explicit the propositions derived from market economics which are, in fact, the deep structure and the regulatory principles of educational change in England and in other societies. In this form they are at least accessible and available for democratic public debate and examination.

These propositions, as mediated by the New Zealand Treasury, consist of four interrelated arguments. The first is that public consciousness, while believing education to be a public good, has a relatively uninformed notion of what a public good is. The second is that economic science can provide a more robust and analytically vigorous concept of a public good to inform debates about educational and social policy. The third is that when the insights of economic science are applied in this way, it becomes apparent that education cannot claim the status of a public good but is in fact a commodity in the market place. The fourth is that state 'intervention' in the provision of education weakens the ability of the market place to generate greater efficiency and equity in education. Language in itself can be a powerful ideological form. The New Zealand Treasury writers' constant use of the language of state 'intervention' implies an artificial intrusion into some natural process (the market). It is necessary in the interests of impartial scholarship to represent these arguments by direct reference to the Treasury brief. The first three arguments are found in interconnected form in the following passage:

> Education's investment benefits, which bring long-term benefits to
> society as well as the individual, may lie behind the feeling that edu-

cation does not belong in the market place. Education tends to be thought of as a natural sphere for government intervention because it is a social or public good and because of concerns about equity in the private costs and benefits flowing from education . . . In the technical sense used by economists, education is not in fact a 'public good' . . . Pure public goods possess the characteristics of being non-exclusive i.e., individuals cannot be excluded from enjoying them (for example, defence): non-competitive i.e., the marginal cost of another individual enjoying the good is zero (for example, an empty railway carriage) and non-positional i.e., the value does not lie in restricted supply (for example, prestige goods) . . . The provision of formal education and the associated educational qualifications does not fall into these categories. Individuals can be excluded from provision and persons outside compulsory school age are excluded. The marginal cost of provision is not zero. The value of educational qualifications does, at least in part, lie in their scarcity. Hence, education shares the main characteristics of other commodities traded in the market place. (New Zealand Treasury, 1987, p. 33)

It may be noted that these arguments are preceded in the Treasury brief by statements which refer to certain weaknesses in public discussion about education e.g.,: 'In the public arena, debate does not seem to have been well focussed on the underlying issues and dilemmas facing the development of education policy' [preface] and statements which suggest that the Treasury economists are bringing some rigour to the field e.g., 'The section on education in Chapter 3 . . . is couched in those terms [economic concepts]. Generally we would consider that such an approach is an analytically robust method which can generate useful insights'. (p. 2)

The strategy employed here, which I have referred to elsewhere (Grace, 1988) as 'ideological manoeuvre', is to suggest that in a field of public policy previously dominated by 'feeling' that education is a public good, robust, technical analysis from economic science can demonstrate that, on the contrary, education is a commodity in the market place.

Once this major conceptual shift has been made, it then becomes possible to think of educational policy and provision in radically different ways. One of the subjects for radical revision can then become the State's responsibilities for education. This in fact constitutes the New Zealand Treasury's fourth argument as expressed in the following passage:

In sum, government intervention is liable to reduce freedom of choice and thereby curtail the sphere of responsibility of its citizens and weaken the self-steering ability inherent in society to reach optimal solutions through the mass of individual actions pursuing free choice without any formal consensus. Government intervention produces its own internal dynamics and hence problems. (ibid., p. 41)

It may be noted here that this robust statement of economic science contains two remarkable assumptions of economics, not as science but as doctrine i.e., that there is such an entity as 'the self-steering ability' and that this entity when operating in a market situation for education will deliver 'optimal solutions'.

As suggested earlier, arguments of this type are implicit in the nature of educational change currently taking place in England and in other societies. Where the economists of the New Zealand Treasury have made a valuable contribution to public debate is by making the concepts, the assumptions and the policy consequences of market-led education very clear. It is at the level of policy consequences for education that this analysis achieves its greatest populist appeal. Once the commodification and marketization of education has been achieved, then consumer sovereignty must be established. The Treasury brief therefore argues: 'the key element . . . is empowering, through choice and through maximising information flows, the family, the parent or individual as the customer of educational sources' (p. 42). This would overcome, in the view of the Treasury economists, the fundamental weakness of the existing system of publicly provided education, that is, 'an unwillingness to empower the consumer'.

Who could disagree with the proposition that, in a democracy, individuals should receive appropriate information about public services? Who could disagree with the proposition that individuals should be empowered by greater involvement in, and decision-making about, such services? The ideological manoeuvre of this particular argument is to suggest that such empowerment can be achieved only by a market place – customer relation rather than by a public service – citizen relation. It is comparatively easy to demonstrate in various societies that citizens have less information about, and involvement in, public services than the ideal of participative democracy entails. Whether this situation would be radically improved by the introduction of a market place – customer relation is partly a matter for empirical investigation. The empirical evidence at this stage is conflicting. Chubb and Moe (1990) and Green (1991) claim considerable successes for market-based school reform in East Harlem. Ball (1993) suggests that, on the contrary, 'the market provides a mechanism for the reinvention and legitimation of hierarchy and differentiation via the ideology of diversity, competition and choice' (p. 16).

It is however not only an empirical matter. To substitute the individual as consumer of education for the individual as citizen in the education service changes more fundamentally the nature of the education process itself. Customers are concerned to maximize private good and individual return in their transactions. The concept of citizen implies a set of wider social and political responsibilities. An obvious danger for education in a market place – customer culture is that issues to do with education for democracy, facilitating equality of educational opportunity and encouraging moral, social and community values could be undermined or at least marginalized. These are clearly areas where education's credentials to be regarded as a public good are strongest and yet in the technical language of economic science these are relegated to the category of 'externalities'. Externalities are defined by economists as arising 'wherever one individual's actions affect the utility of another individual' (Cowen, 1992, p. 2). They refer to the wider social, environmental and political consequences of economic activity (see Tooley, 1993).

It is here that the limitations of modern economic science when compared with classical political economy become most evident. Political economy has always recognized that economic processes and market situations have a crucial relation with wider social, cultural and political characteristics of a society. Modern economic science has often failed to make these crucial connections or at best has marginalized them in the language of externalities. The application of economic science to education often results therefore in analyses which are crude and reductionist and the policy implications which flow from such applications tend to be mechanistic and oversimplified. This is not to say that there cannot be a sensitive and sophisticated study of the economics of education or of its political economy (see Grace, 1988 and 1994). However the forms of economic science which are currently being favoured politically as suitable for application to education policy and practice are crude and reductionist and therefore it is necessary to resist them.

Resisting Economic Science in Education Policy

There are at least two ways in which the domination of economic science in education policy may be resisted. The first is to construct an argument which refuses to accept as definitive or especially authoritative the language, concepts, assumptions and mode of analysis of market economics when applied to education. This form of argument rejects in particular the narrow and mechanistic concepts of public good used in economic science and argues for alternative conceptions of public good which are more appropriate for application in the sphere of education. The second strategy is to engage with economic science on its own terms and to seek to demonstrate that there are internal contradictions and confusions about public-good concepts in the discourse of economic science. If this can be demonstrated then the proposition that economic science is bringing conceptual rigour to a field of public policy lacking such characteristics can be shown to be presumptuous.

The first of these responses may be called that of democratic counter-advocacy and the second that of technical critique. It is argued here that the two taken together construct a powerful resistance to the presumptions and crudities of market economics when applied to education policy and practice.

Democratic Counter-advocacy

I attempted to provide an example of the first response in arguments published under the title 'Education: Commodity or Public Good?' (Grace, 1988,

1989). In essence, my argument in opposition to the case of the New Zealand Treasury was that there were no compelling reasons why the citizens of New Zealand should accept such an analysis and in fact that there were weighty reasons why they should not accept it. In the first place the New Zealand Treasury was attempting to displace an established discourse of education which spoke of 'children', 'achievements' and 'educational process', with a new discourse which spoke of 'inputs', 'outputs' and 'production functions' (New Zealand Treasury, 1987, p. 7). This, it could be argued, would have a profoundly dehumanizing and mechanizing effect upon the operation of the education system.

Secondly, an established democratic consensus in New Zealand that education was a public good which ought to be freely mediated by the State to all citizens was being challenged with the proposition that education was a commodity in the market place. This, it could be argued, would be used as the conceptual basis for the gradual privatization of educational services in New Zealand without any clear mandate from New Zealand citizens that this was desired. Thirdly, that a strong New Zealand tradition that education was 'a right of citizens' was being challenged with the proposition that it was, as a commodity, 'a choice for consumers'. This, it could be argued, had serious consequences for New Zealand's commitments to participative democracy, equity in education and the encouragement of social and community values. In short, the arguments which constituted my inaugural lecture in Wellington called upon the citizens of New Zealand to consider and evaluate the economic-science propositions for education which emanated from the Treasury. To assist in that process of public debate I offered alternative conceptions of education as a public good in schematic form as follows:

> Might not education be regarded as a public good because one of its fundamental aims is to facilitate the development of the personality and the artistic, creative and intellectual abilities of all citizens, regardless of their class, race or gender status and regardless of their regional location? Might not education be regarded as a public good because it seeks to develop in all citizens a moral sense, a sense of social and fraternal responsibility for others and a disposition to act in rational and cooperative ways?
>
> The ultimate foundation for democracy in New Zealand and for a truly participative and intelligent political process in this country depends upon the education of its people and the extent to which they can articulate and feel confident about the rights of citizenship. Insofar as education provides the basic conditions for making democracy possible it has an immediate claim to the status of being a public good . . . (Grace,1988, p. 214)

In the conclusion of this argument I attempted a formal definition of a public good in these terms:

Public goods are intrinsically desirable publicly provided services which enhance the quality of life of all citizens and which facilitate the acquisition by those citizens of moral, intellectual, creative, economic and political competencies, regardless of the individual ability of those citizens to pay for such services. (ibid., p. 218)

In constructing such a definition I have paid particular attention to the economists' criterion of non-excludability as a key characteristic of a public good and therefore to the fundamental issue of requirement to pay and ability to pay. Non-excludability applies when it is not feasible or desirable to exclude individuals or groups from participation in a public good. In this definition, systems of education provided by the State, the local community, the Church or other agencies, without direct charge to the user, can claim the status of a public good.

Many of the arguments which I have used in counter-advocacy would be referred to in the discourse of economic science as involving 'externalities' (See Tooley, 1993). My argument in 1988–89 against the New Zealand Treasury and which I reiterate now is that in the discourse of democratic decision-making, involving citizens and not simply consumers, these matters are not externalities but, on the contrary, centralities. They are centralities for thinking about education for democracy. They are centralities for thinking about equity and equality of opportunity in education, and they are centralities for the shaping of education policy and practice.

Technical Critique

It is possible to say, of course, that to construct alternative conceptions of public good is likely to have less force in public debate and decision-making than confronting economic science, applied to education, in its own terms i.e., within the discourse and theory of economics. James Tooley (1993) has attempted such an approach in his paper 'Education and "Public Goods": Markets versus the State'. Following a detailed examination of the relevant economic literature (Weisbrod 1962; de Jasay 1989; Kiesling 1990; Malkin and Wildavsky 1991; Cowen 1992), Tooley has been able to demonstrate much more internal contradiction and ambiguity in public-goods theory than the *ex cathedra* pronouncements of the New Zealand Treasury economists would lead one to believe. As a result of his examination of public-goods theory, Tooley makes a number of arguments which are relevant to this chapter.

The first is that economists appear to have a continuum with pure public goods (which require state intervention) at one end and private goods (which are the concern of the market) at the other. A considerable debate exists within economics as to the location of various goods and services on this continuum. The second is that in the case of the issue of externalities where 'there are likely to be benefits to the community or society at large of an educated populace, in terms of social cohesion, law and order and economic growth' then economic theory suggests that 'education and schooling could be referred to as an [impure] public good: it is in this sense that we might be able to argue that education needs state intervention to ensure its provision, in order to obtain these externalities'. (pp. 119–20)

The central importance of Tooley's paper is that it explodes the myth that there are authoritative laws of economic science or clear and rigorous concepts which can be applied to educational policy and practice with reliable knowledge of their effects. Tooley has demonstrated that the issues and the concepts are the subject of continuing debate both within economic science and in the wider society. Unfortunately, on this latter point he does not go far enough. Closer examination of one of his sources would have made this point with greater emphasis. In a powerful critique which engages directly with public-goods theory as used in economics, Malkin and Wildavsky (1991) argue that 'disagreement among economists supports our contention that objective criteria do not exist. The evidence shows that there is indeed a wide dispersion of views about what constitutes a public good and what does not'. (pp. 358–9) They conclude, with arguments derived from a technical analysis, which seem to provide, to this writer at least, a strong counter-thesis to the presumptions of some economic scientists in their plans for education:

- 'A public good is one that the public decides to treat as a public good. That there are areas in which we do not want market criteria to prevail is self-evident.'
- 'We have seen that it is impossible to develop a definition of public goods that rests on the technical properties of the thing itself. . . . The flaws in public goods theory allow economists to promote their personal values under the guise of economic "science".'
- 'It is the moveable boundary between public and private that makes it essential to analyse public policy with our values up front, not hidden behind the seemingly technical concept of public goods.' (Malkin and Wildavsky, 1991, pp. 372–3)

It is a cause for some optimism that the domination of technical rationality (in this case economic science) can be resisted not only by direct counter-advocacy but also by reference to analytical manifestations of its own internal contradictions and ideological manœuvres.

On Putting Our Values up Front: Education as a Public Good

As Malkin and Wildavsky (1991) argue, the case for education as a public good must be adjudicated by democratic public discussion and not determined by apparently authoritative experts, whether these are economists, philosophers or educationalists. However, these experts are entitled, of course, to make their informed contribution to such public debate. My own contribution, as an educationalist, has already been outlined in earlier sections of this chapter.

In summary, my position is that education should be regarded as a public good because its free, universal and equal-access provision is fundamental to the generation of other public goods. It is essential for the effective operation of a democratic society and for the enhancement of civic intelligence and participation. It is a powerful source for the nurture of moral, social and community values and responsibilities and for introducing all children to moral and ethical concepts. It represents, through the schooling system, a democratically provided public service for the enhancement of the intellectual and creative potential of all citizens-in-the-making, with a formal commitment that this enhancement process should not be related to the class, race or gender of the student or to his or her ability to pay for it. It is premised upon the social and public value of maximizing the resources of talent in a population in conditions which establish a sense of fairness and of equal opportunity for all in that process. If all of this is not a public good, then what can be?

However, even if these arguments were accepted, the education-market place debate would not be over. It is sometimes argued that even if the case that education is a public good is conceded, it does not necessarily follow that state or public provision of that good is essential. There is, in contemporary economic science, a developing literature which examines arguments for the superiority of private or market provision of public goods (Cowen, 1992). Tooley's (1993) paper ends in these terms:

> The conclusion of this paper is that education is an (impure) public good, in the economist's sense, but that conclusion alone does not tell us whether or not markets, internal or free, are appropriate mechanisms for educational provision. (Tooley, 1993, p. 121)

In a careful review of the issues related to education as a public and private good in America, Levin (1989) concludes 'In summary, a private market would face intrinsic barriers in producing the public outputs of education so fundamental to US democratic society' (p. 229). We shall be in a better position to adjudicate this issue when more empirical studies of the effects of market culture upon the public-good outcomes of education are available. In the light of the previous discussion however, it does seem improbable that market culture which in its operation puts market before community; which necessarily maximizes strategies for individual profit and advantage; which conceptualizes the world in terms of consumers rather than citizens and which marginalizes issues to do with morality and ethics, will be the appropriate culture in which education as a public good can most effectively be provided.

Gerald Grace

Note

1. I would like to acknowledge the help of the librarians of Durham University Library and of its Education Section in providing sources for this chapter. I would also like to thank The University of Sussex, Institute of Continuing and Professional Education, in particular Dr Carolyn Miller (director) and Professor Tony Becher for study facilities.

References

BALL, S.J. (1990) *Politics and Policy Making in Education: Explorations in Policy Sociology*, London, Routledge.

BALL, S.J. (1993) 'Education markets, choice and social class: The market as a class strategy in the UK and USA', *British Journal of Sociology of Education*, 14, 1, pp. 3–19.

CHUBB, J. and MOE, T. (1990) *Politics, Markets and America Schools*, Washington DC, the Brookings Institute.

COWEN, T. (1992) 'Public goods and externalities: Old and new perspectives', in COWEN, T. (Ed) *Public Goods and Market Failures: a critical examination*, New Brunswick, Canada, Transaction Publishers.

CULTURAL STUDIES EDUCATION GROUP (1991) *Education Limited: Schooling and Training and the New Right since 1979*, London, Unwin Hyman.

DALE, R. (1989) *The State and Education Policy*, Milton Keynes, Open University Press.

DE JASAY, A. (1989) *Social Contract, Free Ride: A Study of the Public Goods Problem*, Oxford, Clarendon Press.

GRACE, G.R. (1988) 'Education: commodity or public good?', Inaugural Lecture in Education, Wellington, Victoria University Press.

GRACE, G.R. (1989) 'Education: Commodity or public good?', *British Journal of Educational Studies*, 37, 3, pp. 207–21.

GRACE, G.R. (1994) 'Urban education, democracy and the culture of contentment', in GORDON, P. (Ed) *The Study of Education*, London, Woburn Press.

GREEN, D.G. (Ed) (1991) *Empowering the Parents: How to Break the School's Monopoly*, London, Institute of Economic Affairs.

HILLGATE GROUP (1987) *The Reform of British Education*, London, Claridge Press.

KIESLING, H.J. (1990) 'Pedagogical uses of the public goods concept in economics', *Journal of Economic Education*, Spring, pp. 137–47.

LEVIN, H.M. (1989) 'Education as a public and private good', in DEVINS, N. (Ed) *Public Values, Private Schools*, London, The Falmer Press.

MALKIN, J. and WILDAVSKY, A. (1991) 'Why the traditional distinction between public and private goods should be abandoned', *Journal of Theoretical Politics*, 3, 4, pp. 355–78.

MANSON, H. (Ed) (1992) *New Zealand Annual Review of Education (1991)*, Wellington, Department of Education, Victoria University of Wellington.

McMURTRY, J. (1991) 'Education and the market model', *Journal of Philosophy of Education*, 25, 2, pp. 209–17.

MIDDLETON, S., CODD, J. and JONES, A. (Eds) (1990) *New Zealand Education Policy Today: Critical Perspectives*, Wellington, Allen and Unwin.

NEW ZEALAND TREASURY (1987) *Government Management: brief to the incoming Government (Vol. 2) Education Issues*, Wellington, Government Printer.

SIMON, B. (1992) *What Future for Education?*, London, Lawrence and Wishart.

TOMLINSON, J. (1986) 'Public education, public good', *Oxford Review of Education*, 12, 3, pp. 211–22.

TOOLEY, J. (1993) 'Education and "public goods": Markets versus the state', Paper presented to the Annual Conference of the Philosophy of Education Society of Great Britain, Oxford, New College, April.

WEISBROD, B.A. (1964) *External Benefits of Public Education: An Economic Analysis*, Princeton, Princeton University Press.

Chapter 13

In Defence of Markets in Educational Provision

James Tooley

Introduction

'Markets' are not popular amongst politically correct educationalists. When governments in Britain, Australia, and New Zealand made tentative steps towards introducing 'internal' markets into educational provision, and certain market mechanisms of supply and demand were introduced into state-supplied, state-regulated, and state-funded schooling, they were greeted with howls of disapproval from the educational establishment. Some of this condemnation relates to the ways in which these reforms have been introduced: however what I want to examine in this chapter is not these contingencies, but rather whether educationalists need have any *principled* philosophical objections to markets as such. Thus this chapter is on an abstract level, conducting a 'thought experiment' to isolate what objections there might be.

Some might get impatient with such abstract discussion, claiming that it avoids real issues or fails to contexualize our concerns. However, I get similarly impatient with those who crusade against 'markets' in education, perhaps on the grounds, as we shall see, that education is a 'public good', or that markets won't satisfy 'equality of opportunity', without being clear what is meant by these concepts or how they relate to each other. This argument is abstract because as a philosopher I hope to 'clear the air' so that discussion about practical policies can continue more constructively. But that said, this of course is not the only way to proceed with the argument for markets and against state intervention in education. (I choose the term 'state intervention' carefully, because it emphasizes that before the State got involved educational provision was provided by markets and the other agencies of civil society, and that state intervention *was* an artificial intrusion into this process.) An adequate 'defence' of markets would also need and benefit from historical and empirical work to show both the failures of state intervention in education, the historical successes of non-state educational provision (see West, 1975, High and Ellig, 1992), and benefits of market mechanisms in education and in general (see Chubb and Moe, 1990, and Gray, 1992). My argument complements this other work. It might seem dry by comparison, but then, in some circles in which I mix, 'wetness' is not necessarily a virtue.

Now, just as there is no such thing as a free lunch, there is no such thing as a 'free market'. It is a fiction of the neo-classical economists, which they use to greater or lesser force in predictions of economic behaviour. But there are 'markets' (note plural), with lesser or greater degrees of state intervention, and with lesser or greater imperfections (in terms of information of the consumers, transaction costs, etc). And by 'markets' all I understand is situations where people have property rights to goods and services. Private property rights include individuals' rights to engage with others, on mutually agreeable terms and without interference from third parties, to retain, obtain or dispose of goods and services. They are free to decide upon how these goods and services should be used, provided they do not violate the property rights of others. In terms of education, markets in education would require effective 'demand' from the 'consumers' (through having money or vouchers to pay for education); and a reasonably diverse 'supply' side of schools and other educational opportunities.

Given this background, let us freely invent the following 'market model', to see what lessons we can draw from it, and in particular, what principled objections there might be to it. We have a stable society functioning under the rule of law, where the State is only involved in education in the following ways:

1. It sets the standards (through open discussion and debate) of what is deemed a 'minimum adequate education';
2. It licenses an inspectorate to ensure that educational establishments (and these are of all shapes and sizes) meet these standards;
3. It authorizes established charities to ascertain those families who cannot afford to provide adequate educational opportunities for their children, and provides bursaries to these families to be used in inspected educational establishments. Means-tested vouchers would be an alternative but these are felt to be rather intrusive, and discourage families on the income border from trying to earn more (see Kendall and Louw, 1989, p. 234);
4. It compels those children who are not partaking of the minimum adequate educational opportunities to do so.

In these ways, the State thus takes John Stuart Mill's 'harm principle' seriously, but interprets it in a fairly minimal way (unlike say Feinberg, 1984; or Hughes, 1993, p. 52 and p. 63). Thus this State does not provide schooling at all, and only funds it for those who can't fund themselves, allowing markets and other agencies of civil society (for example, charities, religious groups, communities) to operate in educational provision, but providing a safety-net of last resort for those who are not reached by this provision. Note that a key objection of libertarians to state intervention in welfare generally (including education) is that the expansion of state intervention into these areas has a 'crippling effect' on civil society, by crowding out private initiative (see Hughes, 1993, p. 57).

Given this abstract model, are there any principled objections to such a system? Reviewing the massive recent literature opposing moves towards markets in educational provision, I suggest that there would be three main areas of objection which would carry over to this market model. In addition there might be some incredulity that without the State, educational opportunities could be provided at all; to those who respond in this way, I suggest a look at the history of education in nineteenth-century England and Wales, or America, or even in Scotland (see West, 1970; Gardner, 1984; High and Ellig, 1992; Stephens, 1987). Of course there are historical disputes about the exact numbers in schooling, and the quality of the schooling provided (and some of the writers are guilty of anachronistic judgments about how bad the quality was, given the relative poverty of the society) but no dispute that private interests *were* able to provide schooling for the vast majority. The first intuitively appealing objection might be that education is a 'public good', and therefore schooling and other educational opportunities should be publicly provided. Secondly, it might be argued that the market model could not possibly satisfy 'equality of opportunity'. Finally, it might be felt that the important links between education and democracy would be undermined by such a market system.

Let us turn to the 'public-goods' issue first. Most supporters of this thesis seem content to leave the argument on this intuitively plausible level; however, Gerald Grace (1989) elaborates a detailed defence of the notion that education is a public good and hence should be publicly provided. Can his argument — an argument against the introduction of market mechanisms into educational provision — be used to find principled objections to our market model?

Education As a 'Public Good'

Grace (1989) writes in the context of the debate about internal markets in educational provision in New Zealand, focusing on the arguments of the New Zealand Treasury. Thus he explicitly sets out to challenge *economists'* arguments about 'public goods', with the aim of resisting their conclusions about the role of the State in education.

Economists use the notion of a 'public good' to isolate those goods which will not be provided, or which will be underprovided by markets, so their definition is clearly germane to our task here. These 'public goods' are at the opposite end of a spectrum from 'private goods', or commodities (Mansfield, 1980, p. 80). Thus if education is a public good in this economists' sense, then it would need *state intervention* to ensure its provision; if not, then it won't. I have simplified things somewhat for the purposes of this chapter, for the economists' 'public goods' support a positive, not a normative claim. Public goods will be underprovided without state intervention: this does not say that the State *should* intervene to ensure their provision — to argue that would require additional arguments concerning the value of the public goods in question and why the State can override individual liberty, and so on, in order to impose these goods on people. Conversely, if goods are *not* public goods, then this says that governments *don't need to* intervene to ensure their provision: but this does not rule out that a case could be made as to why governments *should* intervene, even if they don't have to. (For more details along these lines see Tooley, 1993.)

Curiously, it is not altogether clear that Grace's argument could be used against the 'internal market' brought in by the New Zealand government — or likewise the 'internal market' introduced by the British government. For in these 'internal markets' education is still publicly funded through taxation, publicly provided, and publicly regulated. Grace seems to have fallen into the trap of assuming that objections to 'markets' in general can also be used as objections to 'internal markets'. But usefully in the context of *this* chapter, we *are* looking at principled objections to a more 'genuine' market, and hence Grace's objections, if they hold, should be on much stronger grounds. So what is his argument against the economists?

As a preliminary, we note that economists define a public good as satisfying up to three conditions: indivisibility, non-rivalness and non-excludability. The New Zealand Treasury used different terminology, but the same concepts: 'non-competitive' is the same as 'indivisible'; 'non-positional' is the same as 'non-rival'. *Indivisibility* pertains to a good, any given unit of which 'can be made available to every member of the public' (Taylor, 1987, p. 5). For example: a bridge over a river, which can be used by anyone without extra costs being incurred. *Non-rivalness* is virtually the same as this, accept that it is the *benefits* available to every member of the public which are not reduced, rather than the *amount* of the good. A good which is indivisible, then, need not be non-rival, or vice versa. For example, the 'good' of hiking in the Grand Canyon could be, to a large extent, indivisible, in that many millions of people could hike there without thereby hindering others from also hiking there. However, if more than a few people hike there, then this will lower the enjoyment of those who wished to hike in an empty wilderness. Hence in this case, the indivisible good is not non-rival. Finally, *non-excludability* pertains when it is not feasible to exclude any individual members of the group from consuming the good. The classic economic example is of the lighthouse: 'Each shipping company owner knows that if another shipping company erects a lighthouse it will effectively serve his ships as well' (Cowen, 1992, p. 3).

Economists' have their own difficulties with deciding which of these should be the defining features of a public good. All definitions of public goods involve one or more of three conditions, but just about all permutations of these conditions seem to be exhibited somewhere in the literature. For example, McLean (1987) thinks that a public good should exhibit all three qualities (p. 9), as did the New Zealand Treasury. Mueller (1989) says it should only have the first two conditions (p. 11); Leuthold (1987) agrees (p. 58). Kiesling (1990) argues that it is the last two that define a public good (p. 138). Taylor (1987) thinks it is the first and last (pp. 5–6). It turns out however that schooling and the provision of other educational opportunities satisfy *none* of these conditions. Firstly, it is clearly not non-excludable. It is very easy to see how a particular child can be excluded from, for example, a classroom, or refused access to a computer, theatre, cinema or other educational opportunity. Indeed it seems precisely *because* education is excludable in this way that reformers wanted and continue to want the State to be involved in education!

Similarly for non-rivalness and indivisibility. It *is* the case that, for example, if some children have the attention of an excellent teacher, then that teacher has less time for others (indivisibility), and others can obtain less benefit from him or her (non-rivalness). So schooling is not non-rival or indivisible. Again, it seems likely that it was precisely because of this condition that reformers wanted the State to be involved in education, to alleviate this inequality of access. In other words, the irony is that it seems because schooling is *not* a public good in the economists' sense that it could be argued that it needs to be publicly provided!

Grace, however, is unhappy with the conclusion that education is not a public good. Faced with this, he decides that what is needed is an alternative definition of a public good. In fact, curiously, he gives us two different, definitions (Grace, 1989, pp. 214–5 and p. 218). We consider his second only. He says that: 'Public goods are intrinsically desirable publicly provided services which enhance the quality of life of all citizens and which facilitate the acquisition by those citizens of moral, intellectual, creative, economic and political competencies, regardless of the individual ability of those citizens to pay for services' (p. 218).

Now of course Grace, like Humpty Dumpty, is perfectly entitled to define terms in whatever ways he wants (even in two different ways if he wants, although this seems excessive). But there are difficulties which he has not foreseen in so doing. Firstly, his solution is disappointing, for instead of challenging the economists' argument, he simply avoids it. Economists would be perfectly entitled to dismiss Grace's argument as not addressing the issues with which they are concerned. We will see below that there were ways of challenging the economists directly, without sidestepping the issues they raise.

The second problem is deciding what is in the category of Grace's public goods. Does he want it to include what others often include as public goods, services such as sewage treatment, rubbish collection, public transport, or fire-protection services? If they are included under the rubric of his definition(s), then it would have to be because they facilitate the individual in obtaining, or overcoming difficulties in obtaining, aspects of the good life. But then, surely, food, clothing, shelter, parenting, etc. should also be included as public goods? Using his definition(s), virtually everything desirable in a society becomes a public good. Perhaps this is what Grace would want: but this brings us to the third, and major, problem with his redefinition. This is what purpose the definition of public good is supposed to serve. For economists, the purpose is to delineate goods which need state intervention to ensure their provision. So, economists argue:

1. If a good is a public good then it is not amenable to market provision (by definition).
2. Education (in terms of schooling and other educational opportunities) is not a public good;
3. therefore, education is amenable to market provision.

What Grace attempts is to reconstruct this argument as follows:

2*. Education (in terms of schooling and other educational opportunities) *is* a public good;
3*. therefore, education is *not* amenable to market provision.

However, as he has redefined a public good, he cannot fall back on '1' any more, because he no longer has the economists' definition to fall back on! So in order to supplement his argument, he needs an additional clause as to why his definition of a public good has the implication, as with the economists' definition, that a public good is not amenable to market provision. In a moment, we will return to his argument to see if he does bring to light this supplementary information as to why these newly defined public goods need to be publicly provided. But before doing that, let us outline what a more satisfactory rebuttal to the economists' argument could have been, a rebuttal which doesn't sidestep the issues raised.

The alternative argument could have proceeded in two main ways. Firstly, it could have been pointed out that economists get into all sorts of difficulties with their definition, because there might not be *any* public goods in their strict sense at all. Consider, for example, non-excludability. De Jasay (1989) doubts whether any good could be said to be intrinsically non-excludable: 'daylight is excludable by putting coin-operated automatic shutters on windows, allowing access to daylight to be bought by the hour' (p. 61). Malkin and Wildavsky (1991) concur that non-exclusion 'is always a function of the time and resources that the supplier is willing to devote to [exclusion]' (p. 362). A skilful shoplifter, trespasser, or burglar will not allow himself or herself to be excluded from any goods. Even the archetypal 'public good', national defence, (cited almost universally by economists as a public good), can also be excludable. Citizens can exclude themselves from some protection, through, for example, nuclear-free zones; protection can be withdrawn from, or not be extended to, border regions of a nation — topical examples include Iraq's inability to 'defend' the integrity of its territory above the 36th and below the 32nd parallels, and the United Kingdom's inability to defend the Channel Islands from German occupation during World War II. De Jasay

(1989) argues: 'What the exercise teaches is that "excludability" is a variable property of the universe of goods, being reflected in variable exclusion costs. This is a good reason to stop talking about the non-excludability of *public* goods and talk instead of the greater or lesser exclusion costs of goods *in general*' (p. 61).

These considerations suggest that, rather than sidestepping the issue, Grace could have concluded that, although schooling is not a public good in this sense, neither are many other so-called public goods. There might not be any *pure* public goods. To counter this, economists could perhaps argue that their intention is for there to be a continuum, with their pure definition of public good at one end, and private goods at the other, and the majority of goods, perhaps even all goods, in between. They would then argue that as exclusion costs for any good become greater, then it is more likely to need state intervention to ensure its provision: that is, a good with great exclusion costs could be considered an 'impure' public good.

However schooling (and the provision of other educational opportunities) is likely to fail to be even an 'impure' public good. For schooling is likely to have very small exclusion costs or the costs could even be *negative*, that is, there would be educational benefits from exclusion of certain children. (It could be cheaper to get marginal improvement in an average child if those who lack the appropriate skills and background are not allowed to retard the progress of the rest).

A second, more satisfactory, way Grace could have challenged the New Zealand economists on their home territory would be by observing one crucial factor which seems to have been overlooked. Schooling (or the provision of other educational opportunities) does not approach being a public good, definitely not, not even an 'impure' one. But schooling, and education more broadly, is likely to have 'externalities' — defined by economists as when an activity undertaken by one party directly effects another party's utility. That is, there are likely to be benefits to the community or society at large if there are educational opportunities available, in terms of equality of opportunity, social cohesion, democratic benefits, law and order, economic growth, and so on. (For discussion of these externalities — including equality of opportunity — see Weisbrod, 1962.) Crucially, these externalities *do*, in general, exhibit a large degree of non-exclusion (it is not possible or it is costly to exclude people from these benefits or costs) and there are usually considerations of non-rivalness or indivisibility — the external benefits or costs are likely to be available to all with zero marginal costs. For example, a society lacking in equality of opportunity could be a society with a dissatisfied populace, becoming lawless, or lacking in social cohesion. I could exclude myself from the problems of such a society, but only at the great expense of burglar alarms, bodyguards, high fences, or by restricting my movements. It is in this sense that education *could* be referred to as an (impure) public good; it is in this sense that we might be able to argue that education needs state intervention to ensure its provision, in order to obtain these externalities. Moreover, we can now return to Grace's argument, for he gets very close to this formulation when he asks:

> Might not education be regarded as a public good because one of its fundamental aims is to facilitate the development of the personality and the artistic, creative and intellectual abilities *of all citizens regardless of their class, race or gender status and regardless of their regional location?* Might not education be regarded as a public good because it seeks to develop *in all citizens* a moral sense, a sense of social and fraternal responsibility for others, and a disposition to act in rational and co-operative ways? (Grace, 1989, p. 214, my emphasis)

In other words what Grace seems to be saying (note the passages emphasized) is that one reason why the public good of education should be publicly provided is that equality of educational opportunity is important, and that if left to the vagaries of markets, this will not be ensured. Moreover, there could also be the implication that other important 'externalities' of education, such as education for democracy, social cohesion, and so on, will also be underprovided by markets, and hence these are also reasons why education needs to be publicly provided. In other words, by exploring the issue of public goods, we have come full circle to the other fundamental objections to our market model mentioned earlier, that it would not satisfy equality of opportunity, and that links between education and democracy will be broken.

In a chapter of this length, there is not space to address both of these issues: elsewhere I have explored issues concerning education and democracy, and suggested that they do not survive as principled objections to markets (Tooley, 1994). Here, I focus in on the issue of equality of opportunity. I have chosen this issue because it is seen by many to be the easiest way to dismiss markets in education. Markets and inequalities are almost synonymous for many commentators, so tackling the issue of inequality is addressing the opposition to markets where it might be thought to be at its strongest.

Equality of Opportunity through Markets?

It seems intuitively obvious that our market model will not be able to provide equality of opportunity. Markets 'unashamedly' exacerbate inequalities and hierarchies (Clay and Cole, 1991, p. 1). Markets, would 'of course, lead to far greater inequalities of opportunity within the education system' (Levitas, 1986, p. 84). So does the model fall to this challenge? The philosopher's answer to this, of course, is that it all depends what is meant by 'equality of opportunity'. If the words were to be interpreted literally, then we would have to concede the case: for in the market model all that is guaranteed is that everyone has an adequate education; over and above this there is likely to be inequalities of provision, and inequalities of opportunity. But do we need to interpret 'equality' in this literal way? I suggest not, and moreover, that even when philosophers of the political left — those most likely to be objecting to markets — discuss inequality they too don't mean to be taken literally, even when their pronouncements would suggest otherwise. For example, consider the writings of that arch-egalitarian Dworkin: he has written a defence of equality under the helpful title of 'Why Liberals Should Care About Equality'. Even though, unfortunately, nowhere in the article does he explicitly say why this should be the case, there are several hints. For example, he notes that a 'substantial minority of Americans . . . earn wages *below any realistic "poverty line"*' (Dworkin, 1985, p. 208, my emphasis). He asks, is there 'a case for ignoring those *in the economic cellar* now?' (p. 209, my emphasis). But in both these situations, the problem is not that there is inequality as such, but that the minority lives in poverty. He virtually admits as much in the conclusion, when he writes: 'We need not accept the gloomy predictions of the New Right economists that our future will be jeopardized if we try *to provide everyone with the means to lead a life with choice and value*' (p. 212, my emphasis). So he has jumped from trying to show that what is important is that everyone has what might be termed an 'adequate life' (one with choice and value) to that everyone should be equal. This is a luxury not afforded by his argument.

The impression from this argument is that Dworkin would be content, rather than with equality, with some notion of 'adequacy'. Couldn't a parallel notion be given to those who write about equality of educational opportunity — that it is not literal 'equality' they are seeking, but a sense of everyone having access to an *adequate* education? If this could be argued, then clearly the market model outlined above *would* satisfy this sense of 'equality of opportunity': for it is posited on precisely the notion that the educational establishments are inspected to ascertain provision of an adequate education, and that all are allowed access to this by virtue of the state bursaries.

If we examine those philosophers who have written on equality of educational opportunity, this interpretation of what they mean seems plausible enough. For example, Bernard Williams (1962) argues that the old '11+' system of selection to grammar schools in England and Wales was objectionable because middle-class children had more chance of passing the examination than working-class children. I reject the interpretation that in this objection he is arguing that we must make the educational experiences of these classes as equal as possible (*pace* p. 127); instead I suggest that what Williams is objecting to is not that the different children's conditions are unequal, but simply that the working-class child's is *inadequate*, in this case for passing the 11+ examination. Williams's other examples about 'equality' can also be interpreted in this way: his objection to difference in treatment of rich and the poor in terms of health-care (p. 122), is because the 'proper ground of distribution of medical care is ill health' and so those whose needs are the same should receive the same treatment. But is it really the *inequality* of treatment that is of concern to Williams? Surely it wouldn't make any difference on the grounds Williams has given us if the richer person was treated in plush surroundings, with many luxuries, by very eminent highly paid consultants, while the poorer person was treated in a large ward, without any luxuries, by less eminent and hence cheaper medical practitioners, *provided that both treatments were adequate*.

I suggest that we can make analogous comments about educational provision. The 'grounds for distribution' of education would be educational need. Provided that an 'adequate' education was being acquired by all, even extreme inequalities of educational provision would not matter. So Williams, I suggest, could be happy with everyone receiving an 'adequate' education, rather than having 'equality' in any stricter, more literal, sense.

A trickier argument concerning equality of opportunity to address might be that of John Rawls (1972). He extended Williams' argument introducing the complexities of, as is well-known, the social contract and the 'original position'. In the original position, individuals, stripped of the positions in which they would find themselves in society, are able to rationally decide the principles which, if operating, would ensure a fair society (p. 17). Could his argument also be used to support the notion that equality of educational opportunity can be translated to mean 'an adequate education for all', and hence be satisfied by our market model?

At first sight it doesn't seem that it can. For individuals behind the 'veil of ignorance' come up with two principles of justice, the second of which — the 'difference' principle — insists that only those inequalities which 'enhance the opportunities of those with the lesser opportunity' (p. 303) are to be permitted. Within our market model it is unlikely that we would be able to show that the resulting inequalities did satisfy this principle. So if we accept Rawls' 'difference principle', then we would have grounds for rejecting the market model. But is his 'difference principle' inviolable? What are his arguments for it?

Very briefly, Rawls thinks that this principle — together with his other principle of justice — that each person is to have an equal right to the most extensive total system of equal basic liberties compatible with a similar system of liberty for all' (p. 302) — will in combination guarantee a 'satisfactory minimum' standard of living (p. 156), and that without them, any society would involve too 'grave [a] risk' (p. 154). But can such a satisfactory minimum be guaranteed by his principles? Could it not be guaranteed in any other way? Firstly, it is hard to see how Rawls could possibly assume that principles of justice alone could assure the satisfactory minimum. For in a position of ignorance about our society, we don't know 'its economic or political situation, or the level of civilisation and culture it has been able to achieve' (p. 137). So it could be that our society will be one in which there is no-one, for example, with any entrepreneurial, scientific or technological talent, or without productive resources, or lacking opportunities for trading with other nations. It would seem to follow that our society could be incredibly poor, and although we might find it the case that we are all equally free and the inequalities are arranged so that they do benefit the poorest of all, we might find that *no one* has the satisfactory minimum standard, or that only some reach that level. A simple example illustrates some of the difficulties. Let us assume a society with a minimum adequate level of income of £15,000. Three individuals in our society, A, B and C, have incomes of £15,000, £15,000, and £2,000 respectively. Assume that everything about the society satisfies Rawls' two principles of justice throughout. A is permitted to increase her earnings, say by opening a small business, if this will benefit C, the least-advantaged, say by employing him. Suppose the new incomes are A: £20,000; B: £15,000; C: £10,000. We have done everything within Rawls' two principles of justice, and in particular the difference principle. But notice, crucially that C is still living beneath the minimum adequate level. The difference principle has certainly not guaranteed the minimum level for all!

Rawls wanted his two principles of justice to guarantee minimum standards: it seems they do not succeed in doing that. But surely there is a feasible way of guaranteeing this minimum from behind the veil of ignorance: it could be *decided* that this is what is desired of a society: a society, capital (human and material) permitting, with a safety-net, a minimum below which no-one could fall. So this is my suggestion, that such a society would be compatible with what Rawls was seeking from his principles of justice. Moreover, this also seems to be compatible with the restrictions on knowledge imposed by Rawls on individuals behind the veil of ignorance (p. 137). Putting the argument in terms of educational opportunity, then, we could say that compatible with what Rawls was seeking from his difference principle was not *equal* educational opportunity, but a guarantee that everyone should have access to an *adequate minimum* education. Dworkin, Williams and Rawls: all seem as though they should be happy with this conception of equality of educational opportunity.

So, at last, we return to our market model: can our market model satisfy equality of opportunity? If we move away from simple, literal slogans it seems it can. Our model can satisfy giving everyone a 'minimum adequate education'; hence it does satisfy equality of opportunity.

Markets Versus States

Let us recap. What has been achieved from these excursions into public-goods theory and equality of opportunity? We posited an abstract market model in order to see more clearly what principled objections there could be to markets in educational provision. One pat objection is that 'education is a public good', so it cannot be left to markets. Our response was along the lines of 'what do you mean by a public good, and why does that mean that it can't be left to markets?' Having addressed one recent, sophisticated argument along these lines, we concluded that, in terms of its 'externalities', education could arguably fit the bill, in particular, because of the desire for equality of opportunity. However, when we examined the meaning of equality of opportunity, it was suggested that this was not, after all, beyond the reach of our market model. So glib objections — at least the two considered here — to our market model have not succeeded in undermining it.

But non-philosophers, if they have stayed with me this far, might still be wondering what the relevance of all this is for the current debate about markets in education. Why did I go to the extremes of examining the market model outlined earlier? One reason was, as I remarked earlier, that it would allow us to explore principled objections to markets, rather than the contingencies of actual reforms, to allow us to examine whether it is really markets we are objecting to, or something else. But another good reason for going to this extreme is that very often writers from the political 'left' — and Grace is not alone in this — move very quickly from discussion about the 'internal markets' (with, recall, state funding, state regulation and state provision of schooling) to making sweeping judgments about 'free markets': if pressed, they argue that this is because they fear moves to internal markets are preliminary steps along the way to wholesale privatization of education — see for example, the edition of the *British Journal of Educational Studies* devoted to this concern (Volume XXVI, No 1, 1988). So what they fear is that internal markets will lead to real markets, with something like our market model.˙ I have argued that there might not be philosophical objections even to such a market, provided that there was a safety-net to ensure a minimum adequate education for all.

But more than this, I do feel we can use the discussion of our model to examine current, or potential reforms. So, for example, I wrote much of this chapter in South Africa, where there is a perceived need for restitution for the evils of apartheid, coupled with the suspicion in many quarters that giving strong redistributive powers to the State would be unwelcome (South Africans of all races, for good reason, are very suspicious of the power of the State). Some brave souls have put forward proposals that markets could go some way to solving this problem: in education for example, simply divide the total budget spent on schooling by the number of school children, and give each a voucher of that amount, to be spent in licensed educational institutions (Kendall and Louw, 1989, pp. 228–9). In this way, black South Africans would receive roughly twice per capita spending than previously, whites roughly half. Predictably, the cries went up against this solution that 'education is a public good' and such market mechanisms distort this, or that such a market would exacerbate inequalities. I suggest that the arguments of this chapter, suitably modified, can address these concerns. Similarly, in any debate about the virtues of vouchers, or in a more satisfactory development of the internal markets of the Education Reform Act in England and Wales, markets can be defended against principled objections along these lines.

This chapter has, however briefly, defended 'markets' against some of the criticisms levelled against them. But still it might be asked: why argue *for* markets at all, even if they don't suffer from these disadvantages, why would we want them? I believe this question if it occurs to anyone (and it clearly occurs to Grace) should be turned on its head: instead we should ask, why have *state* intervention at all, beyond the minimal levels outlined in the market model? What are the philosophical justifications for state intervention? For state involvement in education is not some 'naturally' occurring phenomenon. State intervention is so firmly entrenched, that many of us find it hard to imagine a society without it, and this blinds us to the possibilities, limiting our vision. But it is worth remembering that states have not become involved in education for particularly edifying reasons. Luther and Calvin inspired the first compulsory state schooling seeing its role as the suppression of dissent and the inculcation of obedience to the established church and the state (Davie, 1990, p. 231). States the world over have jumped on this particular band-wagon; and the experience of recent reforms in the UK is that they are not particularly keen to jump off once on.

Once the argument is put like this, questioning the justification for state intervention, then our market model provides a very powerful way of exam-ining the issues: if states were not involved in education (except in this mini-mal way) what would be the objections to it? What I have attempted to show is that two common objections need not hold. Of course, if state intervention in education is benign, then most people wouldn't bother questioning it. But it has not been found by many to be at all satisfactory, particularly for the already disadvantaged in society; and of course the debate about markets in education has been initiated in part because of dissatisfaction with state school-ing. The question I want to prompt is the wisdom of allowing states into areas of our lives where they have no business, where the agencies of civil society can manage very well without them. My defence of markets against some criticisms is one step toward that nobler aim.

Acknowledgment

This paper was written while I was a visiting lecturer at the University of the Western Cape, Cape Town, South Africa, September–October 1993. I would like to thank Professor Wally Morrow and Nelleke Bak for organizing the visit, my students for helpful feedback, and Fleur de Villiers and De Beers Centenary for funding my travel.

References

CHUBB, J. and MOE, T. (1990) *Politics, Markets and America's Schools*, Washington DC, The Brookings Institution.

CLAY, J. and COLE, M. (1991) 'General Principles for a Socialist Agenda in Education for the 1990s and into the 21st Century', in CHITTY, C. (Ed) *Changing the Future: Redprint for Education*, The Hillcole Group, London, The Tufnell Press.

COWEN, T. (1992) 'Public goods and externalities: Old and new perspectives', in TYLER, C. (Ed) *Public Goods and Market Failures: A Critical Examination*, New Brunswick, Canada, Transaction Publishers.

DAVIE, E. (1990) 'High-quality efficient schooling', in VORHIES, F. and GRANT, R.G. (Eds) *Liberty and Prosperity: Essays in Limiting Government and Freeing Enterprise in South Africa*, Kenwyn, South Africa, Juta and Co.

DWORKIN, R. (1981) 'What is Equality? Part 2: Equality of Resources', *Philosophy and Public Affairs*, 10, 4, pp. 283–345.

DWORKIN, R. (1985) *A Matter of Principle*, Cambridge, Mass., Harvard University Press.

FEINBERG, J. (1984) *Harm to Others: The Moral Limits of the Criminal Law*, New York, Oxford University Press.

GARDNER, P. (1984) *The Lost Elementary Schools of Victorian England*, London, Croom Helm.

GRACE, G. (1989) 'Education: Commodity or public good?', *British Journal of Educational Studies*, 37, 3, pp. 207–11.

GRAY, J. (1983) 'Classical Liberalism, positional goods, and the politicisation of poverty', in KUMAR, K. and ELLIS, A. (Eds) *Dilemmas of Liberal Democracies: Studies in Fred Hirsch's Social Limits to Growth*, London, Tavistock Publications.

GRAY, J. (1992) *The Moral Foundations of Market Institutions*, Choice in Welfare No. 10, London, IEA Health and Welfare Unit.

HIGH, J. and ELLIG, J. (1992) 'The private supply of education: Some historical evidence', in TYLER, C. (Ed) *Public Goods and Market Failures: A Critical Examination*, New Brunswick, Canada, Transaction Publishers.

HUGHES, K. (1993) 'False antithesis: The dispute about the market and the State', in LIPTON, M. and SIMKINS, C. (Eds) *State and Market in Post Apartheid South Africa*, Johannesburg, Witwatersrand University Press.

DE JASAY, A. (1989) *Social Contract, Free Ride: A Study of the Public Goods Problem*, Oxford, Clarendon Press.

KENDALL, F. and LOUW, L. (1989) *Let the People Govern*, Ciskei, Amagi Publications.

KIESLING, H.J. (1990) 'Pedagogical uses of the public goods concept in economics', *Journal of Economic Education*, 21, pp. 137–47.

LEUTHOLD, J.H. (1987) 'A public goods experiment for the classroom', *Journal of Economic Education*, 18, pp. 58–65.

LEVITAS, R. (1986) 'Competition and compliance: The utopias of the new right', in LEVITAS, R. (Ed) *The Ideology of the New Right*, Cambridge, Polity Press.

MALKIN, J. and WILDAVSKY, A. (1991) 'Why the traditional distinction between public and private goods should be abandoned', *Journal of Theoretical Politics*, 4, 3, pp. 355–78.

MANSFIELD, E. (1980) *Economics: Principles, Problems, Decisions*, 3rd ed., New York, W.W. Norton.

MCLEAN, I. (1987) *Public Choice: An Introduction*, Oxford, Basil Blackwell.

MUELLER, D. (1989) *Public Choice II*, Cambridge, Cambridge University Press.

RAWLS, J. (1972) *A Theory of Justice*, Cambridge, Mass., Harvard University Press.

STEPHENS, W.B. (1987) *Education, Literacy and Society 1830–70: The Geography of Diversity in Provincial England*, Manchester, Manchester University Press.

TAYLOR, M. (1987) *The Possibility of Cooperation*, Cambridge, Cambridge University Press.

TOOLEY, J. (1992) 'The prisoner's dilemma and educational provision: A reply to Ruth Jonathan', *British Journal of Educational Studies*, 40, 2, pp. 118–33.

TOOLEY, J. (1993) 'Education and "public goods": markets versus the state', Paper presented to the Annual Conference of the Philosophy of Education Society of Great Britain, New College, Oxford, April.

TOOLEY, J. (1994) 'E.G. West and State Intervention in Education: A Philosophical Exploration', Unpublished Ph.D. thesis, University of London.

James Tooley

WEISBROD, B.A. (1962) *External Benefits of Public Education*, Princeton, Princeton University Press.
WEST, E.G. (1970) *Education and the State*, 2nd ed., London, Institute of Economic Affairs.
WEST, E.G. (1975) *Education and the Industrial Revolution*, London, B.T. Batsford.
WILLIAMS, B. (1962) 'The idea of equality', in LASLETT, P. and RUNCIMAN, W.G. (Eds) *Philosophy, Politics and Society*, Oxford, Basil Blackwell.

Chapter 14

Politics, Markets and Schools: The Central Issues

Terence H. McLaughlin

The general arguments for and against the salience of market considerations in education are well known (for arguments broadly in favour of markets in education see, for example, Chubb and Moe, 1990, 1992; Coons and Sugarman, 1978; Cox *et al.*, 1986; Flew, 1987; Green, D 1991; Seldon, 1986; Tooley, 1992a, 1992b, 1993a, 1993b, 1993c. For arguments broadly against see, for example, Ball, 1990, 1993; Grace, 1989; Green, A, 1991; Institute for Public Policy Research, 1993; Jonathan, 1989, 1990, 1993; McMurtry, 1991; Miliband, 1991).

My aim in this chapter is to focus attention upon a core of central issues which lie at the heart of the debate about markets in education, to locate them in broader contexts of reference and to encourage further exploration of them, rather than to review all of the arguments in a complex literature. In my discussion I shall make some reference to other contributions to this volume, again not for purposes of review, but to explore relationships with the themes with which I am concerned.

An adequate assessment of the proper role of markets in the determination of educational policy and practice requires complex judgments to be made of both an empirical and an evaluative kind. Here, as with most educational questions, empirical and evaluative questions are related to each other in an intricate way. For example, claims that market systems in education work more effectively than others beg the question of what is to count as effectiveness in this context. On the other hand, the significance of market considerations in education cannot be judged simply by abstract considerations of evaluative principle. Educational principles and values must be realized in practice with particular groups of students and parents in specific institutions and social contexts, subject to forces and influences of many kinds, not least economic and political ones.

In this chapter I shall focus attention in particular on some fundamental evaluative (and more specifically philosophical) questions relating to markets in education. I shall be referring throughout to school education for young people up to the age of around 16 years; the typical minimum school-leaving age in many countries. Other areas of education, for example the organization and funding of higher education, give rise to wider questions.

The Influence of Markets in Education: The Question of Scope

John McMurtry has argued that there is deep contradiction between the aims and processes of education on the one hand and those of the market on the other, and he develops his argument by reference to their opposing goals, motivations, methods and standards of excellence (McMurtry, 1991). Considerations such as those adduced by McMurtry underpin the wide-ranging aversion to any kind of market influence in education felt by some educationalists, who see it as inherently corrosive of educational values wherever it is to be found.

However, a more common focus of debate arises not from a determination to exclude market considerations from education completely but from a recognition that they might have a legitimate *scope* of influence. Crucial issues for debate then become the determination of the nature and extent of this scope, and the justification of the limits drawn.

Discussion of these matters requires a rejection of overly general conceptions of educational markets and their influence, and the need to make important distinctions. One such distinction is between 'internal' and 'free' educational markets. Internal educational markets are those in which the market functions within an overall system in which the State or government retains an important role (for example, in the funding of education through taxation, and in provision and regulation). In contrast, in completely free educational markets, no significant state or government role remains. As is widely recognized, the educational reforms in England and Wales since the 1988 Education Act have, in virtue of a number of prominent features, established an internal, and not a free, market.

Another distinction concerns the differing aspects of education over which control can be exercised. John White, in his contribution to this volume, outlines three such aspects: the determination of the aims and curricula of schooling; the ownership and organization of schools; and the control over admission to schools.

The significance of such distinctions for arguments concerning the legitimate scope of educational markets is clear. Objections to a free educational market, for example, require nuanced reconsideration in relation to an internal market, and objections to market control over the fundamental aims, values and purposes of education do not, at least without further argument, translate into objections to market control of all aspects of their institutionalization in schools.

A full delineation of the proper scope of educational markets cannot be attempted here. However, a number of matters of broadly philosophical principle are relevant to this task, and I shall seek to illuminate these in what follows.

Markets in Education: A Legitimate Sphere of Influence

Few deny that market forces have a degree of legitimate influence in education. One of the potentially least contentious areas of influence concern certain aspects of the efficiency of educational institutions and systems.

As mentioned above, notions such as 'efficiency' cannot be regarded as value-free. However, not all values related to 'efficiency' are (or should be) significantly controversial. Some of the contributions to Part 1 of this volume, for example, describe market influences which have liberated schools and teachers from bureaucratic constraints and introduced a beneficial antidote to institutional stagnation and complacency. As Geoff Morris points out in his contribution, not all market influences upon local education authorities have been educationally detrimental.

The task of discerning the scope of the legitimate influence of market forces, is, however, difficult. Part of the difficulty lies in the complexity inherent in relevant empirical matters. Differences of interpretation of, say, the likely effects of certain administrative policies explain in part the contrasting views of Geoff Morris and Rosalie Clayton, in their contributions in this volume, on the question of the continuing value and importance of local education authorities in the light of the development of grant maintained schools. One aspect of complexity in this kind of dispute is uncertainty arising from a general inability to predict the precise effects of practical policies and the course of future related political and other decisions. Such complexities, viewed as part of the insuperable limitations of relevant human knowledge, form part of the 'epistemic' argument for markets in general (see Gray, 1992, pp. 5–17).

However, not all disputes about the contribution of market forces to the efficiency of educational institutions and systems have the character of empirical or technical disagreements among people who share the same educational aims and values. For example, implicit in Chubb and Moe's discussion of the negative effects of bureaucratic influence upon public schools in the United States is a vision of the family (and specifically parents) as having a radically dominant position in educational decision-making. Of the existing forms of democratic control of US schooling, and the role of families and parents within them, Chubb and Moe complain '. . . even in a perfectly functioning democratic system, the public schools are *not meant* to be theirs to control and are literally *not supposed* to provide them with the kind of education they might want. The schools are agencies of society as a whole, and everyone has a right to participate in their governance. Parents and students have a right to participate too. But they have no right to win' (Chubb and Moe, 1990, p. 32, emphases in original). It is precisely this 'right to win' which Chubb and Moe seek to embed in their educational proposals. Such evaluative commitments, and the disputes to which they give rise, are prominent features of the debate between advocates of market forces in education and their critics. They are also at the heart of the attempt to specify the limits of such forces.

What are the central matters of educational value at stake here? I shall approach this matter by reference to wider debate about the moral limits of the market.

The Moral Limits of the Market

It is widely recognized that the market, and the 'enterprise culture' more generally, has moral significance and implications, and stands in need of evaluation and defence in moral terms (on these matters see Heelas and Morris, 1992).

Morally sensitive discussions of the market cannot fail to acknowledge the notion of moral limits to the scope of its power and influence. As Raymond Plant implies, these limits are related in a complex way to '. . . the range of social and political institutions within which markets are embedded, the scope and purposes of these institutions, and their relationship to the market economy, (and) the debate about the scope of the market and the range of goods which ought to be treated as commodities' (Plant, 1992a, pp. 119–20). For my purposes, I shall draw out, in a rather artificial and abstract way for purposes of discussion, two general limits which are rich in educational implication.

The first of these I shall call the 'civic-virtue' limitation. Forms of civic virtue or Hegelian *Sittlichkeit* are clearly needed to complement, underpin and correct the values of a democratic capitalist society. Michael Novak, in his well-known and wide-ranging moral defence of the market, and democratic capitalism more generally (Novak, 1991, 1993) admits that although a market economy is necessary to political democracy, it requires a particular moral-cultural base; the 'commercial virtues' need 'taming and correction' by '. . . a moral-cultural system independent of commerce' (Novak, 1991, p. 121). There is a need, for example, for a democratic society to secure '. . . the practical substructure of cooperative social life' (ibid., p. 65). A severely practical way of putting a central aspect of this point is that the market cannot survive without the moral (as distinct from merely coercive) underpinning of practices such as the making of contracts. But there are deeper communal needs of society which may be unsatisfied and corroded by aspects of the 'enterprise culture' (on these see, for example, Hollis, 1989, 1990, 1992; Milligan and Watts Miller, 1992). One of the key matters of contention here is the extent to which a concern for social justice can be regarded as part of this 'civic virtue'.

The second moral limit on markets I shall designate the 'personal-autonomy' limitation. Novak's view contains an emphasis on personal autonomy and liberty as a key element in his justification of democratic capitalism, as seen in his claim that the defence of the free market is a defence of the free conscience (Novak, 1991, p. 112). But the claim that the personal autonomy of individuals has a central justificatory role in relation to the market economy, and that it should act as a source of limitation on its scope, is given particularly interesting expression for our purposes in some recent work by John Gray, in both *The Moral Foundations of Market Institutions* (Gray, 1992) and other writing (Gray, 1993).

Gray grounds the ethical significance of market institutions squarely in their contribution to autonomy '. . . one of the vital ingredients of individual well-being in the modern world' (Gray, 1992, p. 2). Unlike classical liberals, Gray sees negative liberty, freedom from coercion, as merely one element of autonomy, properly understood. For in his view, negative freedom only has value in the light of its contribution to the 'positive liberty' of autonomy. Gray describes autonomy as '. . . the condition in which a person can be at least part author of his life, in that he has before him a range of worthwhile options, in respect of which his choices are not fettered by coercion and with regard to which he possesses the capacities and resources presupposed by a reasonable measure of success in his self-chosen path among these options' (ibid., p. 22). The contribution of negative liberty to autonomy understood in this way is therefore clearly partial and incomplete; the inability of an individual to achieve objectives and purposes may not be due to coercion but to the lack of relevant capacities and opportunities. This important point provides a ground for 'positive claims' on the part of individuals to '. . . a decent array of worthwhile options and . . . entitlements to resources' (ibid., p. 30) and hence to the notion of an 'enabling welfare state' (ibid., Ch. 6) which provides a guarantee of '. . . the resources and opportunities required for the autonomous pursuit of the good life . . .' (ibid., p. 57). This last remark seems to open the door to extensive, and perhaps unlimited, welfare-state provision. Gray reins in this implication in a number of ways; for example, by confining the 'guarantee' to matters of *basic needs* remaining unmet by elements of civil life such as the family, charitable organizations and self-provision; by limiting welfare claims through characterizing these basic needs (including autonomy) as *satiable*, so that when the need is met the claim lapses, and by grounding welfare benefits as valid claims to the satisfaction of such satiable basic needs and not in terms of 'rights' and 'justice'.

Although the details of Gray's conception of a 'framework' government with limited positive responsibilities need not concern us here (for critical appraisals of Gray's overall view see Kukathas, 1992; Plant, 1992a), it is important to note that he interestingly brings together in his account both the 'civic virtue' and the 'personal autonomy' sources of moral limitation on market institutions. For Gray, a liberal regime concerned to support the growth of the autonomy of its subjects cannot avoid paying attention to, and assuming some responsibility for, the features of the common environment in which autonomy is exercised (ibid., Ch. 7 and 1993, Ch. 2, 4). Indeed, he is willing to describe such ingredients of a worthwhile form of common life as a species of 'public good' (1993, pp. 13–14, 111, 134; see the debate between Gerald Grace and James Tooley in this volume). Gray describes the 'animating values' of his 'enabling welfare state' as '. . . autonomy, human solidarity and community' (1992, p. 62).

The major interest in Gray's position for our purposes lies in its specification, by a thinker who is hospitable to the market, of two major sources of moral limitation on its operation. The precise implications of such limitations are, of course, complex and cannot be explored generally here. I turn now, however, to their application in the context of education.

Education and the Moral Limits of the Market

Few proponents of market forces in education deny that *some* limits must be placed on the operation of the educational market. Even advocates of 'free' educational markets typically postulate minimum standards which schools must meet and which the State is seen has a role in enforcing.

What limits arise for the educational market, however, from the kinds of moral limits on markets in general which have just been outlined? The potential educational implications of these limits are immediately apparent, for education can play a crucial role in the promotion of both civic virtue and personal autonomy. The precise character of this role depends, of course, on how 'civic virtue' and 'personal autonomy' are to be understood.

To sketch matters roughly, minimal conceptions of civic virtue stress such features of basic social morality as respect for the law and the formal processes of democracy, whereas maximal notions embody a much fuller sense of the forms of civic agency and moral environment required by a liberal democratic society. The notion of minimal and maximal conceptions of personal autonomy has already been illuminated by the distinction between negative and positive conceptions of liberty. At first sight, Gray's argument in *The Moral Foundations of Market Institutions* (Gray, 1992) seems to encourage a maximalist reading of his interpretation of these matters.

The contrast between minimal and maximal conceptions of civic virtue and personal autonomy are related to parallel contrasts between minimal and maximal educational requirements for their realization (see McLaughlin, 1992a). A minimal view of civic virtue and personal autonomy is compatible with an education and schooling system controlled by a light regulatory framework within which many forms — and indeed conceptions — of schooling can flourish in the light of market forces. This is because no substantial educational entitlement for pupils can be derived from minimal notions of civic virtue and personal autonomy. Basic literacy and numeracy, for example, might be sufficient in such a minimal view to enable pupils to understand the demands of the law and the procedures of democracy. Quite clearly, however, maximal conceptions of civic virtue and personal autonomy do indeed generate such a substantial entitlement, consisting of wide-ranging forms of

knowledge and understanding and the development of virtues and dispositions of a complex kind related to democratic citizenship and personal autonomous agency in a fuller sense. Such an entitlement can be variously characterized
in philosophical terms (see, for example, Gutmann, 1987; White, 1990), and
is discernible not only in philosophical treatments, but also, at least in outline,
in policy statements. For example, in its recent 'alternative White Paper' the
Institute for Public Policy Research (Institute for Public Policy Research, 1993,
pp. 7–18) outlines an educational vision which includes the development in all
pupils of a '. . . powerful mixture of intellectual and personal traits. . .' (ibid.,
p. 9) related to positive freedom from constraints of ignorance and personal
resource required both for well-informed and critical democratic citizens, and
for the creation of a society which recognizes '. . . the interdependence of
people and the social richness on which each individual draws' (ibid., p. 17)
(see also O'Hear, P. and White, 1991). Gerald Grace's argument in his contribution to this volume clearly invokes an educational vision of this general
kind.

The notion of an educational entitlement of this sort is very significant
for the question of markets in education because, if justified, it establishes a
criterion by which an adequate education can be judged. The central issue
between advocates and critics of markets in education then becomes: Which
system can best ensure the provision not of some unspecified 'good' or
'adequate' education, whose definition is itself determined by the market, but
of this entitlement? Given the relationship of this entitlement to fundamental
matters of democratic agency and personal dignity, the *prima facie* moral duty
of extending it to all children becomes clear. The question then becomes:
Which system can best ensure the provision of this entitlement for *all*
children?

Can an educational market adequately ensure this provision? The claim
that a totally, or significantly, free market can achieve this is counter-intuitive.
This is not only because of the egalitarian impulse which is part of the requirement of the entitlement, but also because of difficulties in claiming that 'customers' are in a position to seriously evaluate such an entitlement for purposes
of choice, a point illuminated by the discussion by Colin Wringe, in his
contribution to this volume, of the inapplicability of the principle of *caveat
emptor*. James Tooley's argument that the institutions of civil society are sufficient to develop autonomy requires much fuller defence (Tooley, 1993a, pp.
20–2). There seems to be a strong case for exempting the entitlement, if not
other aspects of educational provision, from market forces, and securing its
achievement for all pupils through forms of democratic state control and
regulation. This is the position taken by John White in his contribution to
this volume, although as he emphasizes there and in other writing it is crucial
to note that the argument relates only to states committed to democratic
values and principles. This broad position is arguably also implicit in recent
educational reforms in England and Wales, although the National Curriculum
and its associated assessment arrangements have not been formed in the light

of any very clearly articulated view of the rationale for the entitlement (see White, 1990, Ch. 1, 8 and 1993; O'Hear and White, 1991; King and Reiss, 1993; compare O'Hear, 1993).

What educational implications does John Gray derive from his recognition of the moral limits of the market? Gray acknowledges a class of welfare benefit which is designed to prepare people for '. . . the status of autonomous individuals in a liberal civil society' (Gray, 1992, p. 65). Since he recognizes that the capacity for rational deliberation and choice (ibid., p. 26), is a constitutive element in autonomy, and part of the positive capacities which it involves, Gray seems to be confronted not only with the claim that education is a welfare benefit, but also, given a maximalist reading of his position, with the demand that education involves a substantial educational entitlement of the sort outlined above, and, to ensure its realization, a restriction of the scope of market forces.

Such demands do not, however, find recognition in Gray's educational proposals (Gray, 1993, pp. 27–9, 58, 162–6). These include a wholesale privatization of the schooling system (with state funding being confined to vouchers to supplement very low incomes and a system of merit bursaries for the brightest) and a restricted National Curriculum and assessment arrangements. Gray moves even further away from the notion of a substantial educational entitlement by calling into question the need for compulsory schooling at all, if basic skills can be acquired in other ways (for example in 'skill centres') and in suggesting a reduction in the school-leaving age as an incremental move in this direction.

There seems, at least on the face of it, to be a major inconsistency between Gray's account of the grounds of the moral limits of the market and his educational proposals. Some elements of his proposals seem to hint at the need for a stronger regulatory framework; for example his acknowledgment of the need for courses in civic or political education and the dangers of undue emphasis upon vocationalism in schooling (Gray, 1993, pp. 61) and in his recognition of the need for '. . . a culture of responsibility and choice-making . . .' (ibid., p. 64) to be transmitted to the next generation. Such hints can also be seen in Gray's insistence that Muslim schools should offer equal educational opportunities to both sexes as a condition for receiving state funding (ibid., p. 58).

This inconsistency between an apparent commitment to maximalist interpretations of notions such as personal autonomy and subsequent educational proposals is a feature of the arguments of a number of other defenders of market forces in education (see Cohen, 1981; Coons and Sugarman, 1978). In the case of Gray, at the heart of the inconsistency is a failure to give a satisfactory account of the notion of autonomy.

Raymond Plant bases his criticism of this account on a rejection of Gray's claim that autonomy is a basic satiable need. Satiability, it will be recalled, plays an important role in Gray's attempt to prevent his argument from being dragged in a social market or socialist direction. But Plant rightly points out the profound difficulties inherent in claiming that the need for autonomy can be satiated (Plant, 1992a, pp. 127–32). Involved in such a claim is a judgment about what is to be regarded as a reasonably autonomous life. But who is to decide this, and on what grounds? Plant's own view is that a democratic consensus needs to be sought on such matters. Given resource constraints, autonomy for all citizens in a liberal democracy must be secured on the basis of distributive fairness rather than satiability. For Plant, the 'fair value of liberty' must be secured for individuals through rights to resources which may not be provided in the market (ibid., p. 137; for Plant's general position see also Plant and Barry, 1990; Plant, 1992b; on the notion that the just distribution of educational goods involves an independent sphere of justice, and an internal logic and independent set of distributive processes see Walzer, 1983). This general line of argument provides a foothold for the argument about the moral limits of the educational market which has been outlined above, with its requirement that a substantial entitlement be insulated from market forces. Although much more needs to be said in defence of this argument, our discussion of Gray's position has demonstrated how difficult it is to resist this foothold once even a preliminary acknowledgment of the significance of positive liberty has been conceded.

Challenges to the Moral Limits of the Educational Market

Such an argument will not, of course, carry weight with thinkers of a classical liberal persuasion who resolutely insist upon minimalist views of the moral limits to markets generally (see, for example, Hayek, 1960). An adjudication of fundamental challenges of this kind requires a wide-ranging discussion.

However, even if a maximalist interpretation of the moral limits of the market is adopted, or at least seriously entertained, it by no means follows that the articulation and defence of the notion of moral limits to the educational market is unproblematic. This task of articulation and defence faces a range of significant challenges of various kinds. In this section of the chapter, I shall examine four challenges to the notion of moral limits to the educational market which have a philosophical dimension. These challenges assert in turn: the impossibility of justifying a single substantial educational entitlement in the face of the irremediable diversity of educational aims and values; the negative consequences for the well-being of schools arising from the attempt to impose 'higher-order' aims upon them; the unacceptability of restrictions on parental rights, and the difficulty of demarcating the non-market from the market spheres of influence in education. These challenges, which need not all necessarily arise from a fundamental rejection of the perspective under consideration, usefully indicate some important issues which require attention if it is to be given an adequate defence.

The first challenge involves the claim that educational aims and values are matters of irreconcilable dispute. In the face of this deep-seated diversity of view, which may be seen as extending to the notions of civic virtue and personal autonomy themselves, it is claimed that it is impossible to specify a maximal, as distinct from a minimal, educational entitlement for all pupils. In insisting upon such an entitlement, the democratic state stands accused of imposing a particular educational vision and its related values upon children and parents in a way that is incompatible with the pluralism and freedom that is properly part of a liberal democratic society. To use the terminology employed by Colin Wringe in his contribution to this volume, on what grounds can the State impose a 'vanguard' as distinct from a 'service' conception of education?

A stress on the diversity of educational values, and a concern that the State might use the schooling system for purposes of illicit influence is a recurring theme among defenders of educational markets. Gray expresses the anxiety that schools might become subservient to the 'ephemeral goals' of the government of the day, which underpins his insistence that schools be seen as autonomous institutions, with their own internal ends and purposes (Gray, 1993, pp. 61–2).

The search for agreement about the nature of an educational entitlement has important social, political and practical aspects as well as philosophical ones. The philosophical challenge is, however, important and severe. A very widely adopted general line of response to the challenge is to claim that, if the educational entitlement is concerned with essential civic virtues and the acquisition by pupils of intellectual and personal resources related to their development of autonomy, then the educational ideal involved is essentially an 'open' one, deeply consonant with, and indeed required by, liberal democratic values and not open to serious objection, except from those who explicitly do not value the democratic and autonomous life. Such an ideal is indeed non-neutral, but aspires to be fair and non-repressive in matters of significant controversy.

To command assent, or at least a significant degree of it, such an ideal requires very considerable articulation and defence, including sensitivity to such matters as the scope of liberal values and the proper identification of matters of legitimate diversity (on Rawls' recent thoughts on these matters, which are of considerable educational significance, see Rawls, 1993). There is also an important need for the achievement of a democratic consensus concerning the implications of the ideal in practical terms (on this see, for example, McLaughlin, 1992a). This requires a public climate of debate about educational matters rather different from the one which has prevaled in recent years.

The provision of a philosophical justification for the notion of a substantial educational entitlement insulated from market forces is rendered more difficult by the undermining of lines of justification familar in recent years which are based on a confident invocation of the concept of 'reason' (on this see, for example, Carr, 1994; Hirst, 1993). A justification of an appropriate sort is, however, clearly required if the notion of moral limits to the educational market is itself to be provided with a justification.

The second challenge draws attention to the negative consequences for the well-being of schools arising from the attempt to impose 'higher-order' aims upon them. Chubb and Moe, in *Politics, Markets and America's Schools* (Chubb and Moe, 1990) reject the acceptability of a degree of market facilitated choice coexisting alongside democratic control. They insist that only the full market choice system which they favour, excluding such control, has the capacity to bring about the kind of transformation of schools that is needed (for their criticisms of recent educational reforms in England and Wales on this ground see Chubb and Moe, 1992). The argument here is not a contingent one about the operation of mechanisms of democratic control in a particular context, but is rooted in their perceptions about the very nature of democratic control itself. The *raison d'être* of democratic control over education is to impose 'higher-order values' on schools and therefore to limit their autonomy (1990, p. 38). If these aims are to have a non-platitudinous character, they must be formulated clearly and their implementation assured. The pursuit of these objectives leads, inevitably, however, into precisely the forms of extensive educational bureaucratization which Chubb and Moe identify as the enemy of school effectiveness. This is for two main reasons. First, educational ideals are formulated in the context of the '. . . perpetual struggle for the control of public authority' (ibid., p. 29), in which 'The winners get to use public authority to impose their policies on the losers' (ibid., p. 28). Given the fragility of tenure of any given holder of public authority, and the controversiality of educational aims, there is a tendency for those in authority to seek to protect their policies from being undermined by future power-holders by bureaucratic strategies. Second, such strategies are needed in order to ensure that the aims are implemented by principals and teachers who may not share them and may take advantage of the '. . . widespread incentives and opportunities for non-compliance . . .' (ibid., p. 40). Eric Bolton notes that educational legislation must be specific rather than vague if it is to have any force (Bolton, 1993, pp. 47–8).

The reply to this challenge is in part related to the successful provision of the sort of clarification and justification of fundamental educational vision, and the achievement of significant consensus which the first challenge calls for. This would help to ameliorate the instabilities of political discussion relating to education, and enable, perhaps, a number of central educational principles and values to be lifted out of party political debate. Given this degree of consensus there seems to be no reason why 'higher-order aims' should not be brought to bear effectively on schools without the consequences which Chubb and Moe describe.

The third challenge announces the unacceptability of restrictions on parental rights arising from the notion of a substantial educational entitlement. Elsewhere, I have argued that, although a perspective embodying an entitlement of this kind cannot licence unlimited parental moral rights over their children's education, more wide-ranging parental rights (concerning, for examples, choice of certain sorts of separate school) can be argued to be compatible with this perspective than is sometimes recognized (McLaughlin, 1992b, 1994). This should help to meet, at least to some extent, the concerns expressed in the challenge. The challenge also gives rise to the need to give clear expression to the nature and justification of the notion of the common school within the perspective under discussion.

The fourth challenge raises the difficulty of demarcating the non-market from the market spheres of influence in education. There are clear difficulties in the suggestion that only the aims and curriculum of schools should be immune from market forces. John White, in his contribution to this volume, rightly draws attention to the difficulty of separating out control over aims and curricula from control over such matters as school ownership, organization and admissions. The achievement of a substantial educational entitlement is in part connected with matters of school organization, for example. Given a commitment to such an entitlement, there is a need to assess carefully the effect that market forces might have on the overall educational experience of teachers and children. Certainly many aspects of education do not sit easily with the general ethos of the market (see, for example, Hogan, 1993; Haldane, 1992). A very general anxiety is the potentially corrosive and commodifying effect of the language of the market on educational values and purposes, as in the use of terms such as 'delivery', 'output', 'enterprise' and the like. An overall evaluation of this danger should take into account the capacity of teachers to interpret such language elastically, and to domesticate it to properly educational ends (for an example of this process in relation to the concept of 'enterprise' see Bridges, 1992; compare Bailey, 1992).

This process of adaptation is less easy to engage in when the structure of the educational system is at issue, where policies, in view of their structural character, have an unavoidable effect on all those involved. This is of particular significance when matters of distributive justice are involved (Jonathan, 1989, 1990, 1993). One aspect of this is the fact that at least significant aspects of education can be regarded as positional goods. A good is positional if it is valuable to some people only on condition that others do not have it (Hollis, 1982, p. 236). Hollis notes that schools inevitably differentiate and rank and there are positional elements even in such aspects of the 'nurture of the soul' as talent, culture and virtue. This underscores the need for the educational structure as a whole, and not just its aims and curriculum, to be subjected to careful assessment with regard to the adequacy of market forces in securing the educational entitlement for all pupils. There is a clear egalitarian impulse in such an entitlement, as reflected in Tawney's remark that it is part of a teacher's honour to serve educational needs without regard to the 'vulgar irrelevancies' of class and income (quoted in Walzer, 1983, p. 202). Whilst egalitarianism may be rejected in favour of the achievement of an adequate standard by all (Tooley, 1993c) the notion of an 'adequate standard' on the 'substantial entitlement' view has a considerable egalitarian resonance.

Another aspect of the need for widening the scope of the assessment of market forces in education beyond matters of aims and curriculum concerns the question of how far the conception of parents and the local community as partners in the educational process is undermined by market-dominated relationships.

An acknowledgment of the force of this challenge does not, however, lead to the conclusion that market forces should have no legitimate sphere of influence, even if the precise character of that sphere requires complex contextual judgment.

Conclusion

In this chapter, I have attempted to focus attention upon some central issues relating to markets in education: Are there moral limits to markets in general and to educational markets in particular? What is the nature and justification of these limits? What challenges confront an attempt to delineate them?

I have given support to the claim that considerations relating to civic virtue and to personal autonomy constitute (broadly) moral limits on markets and on educational markets. These two sources of limitation underpin the notion of a substantial educational entitlement for all pupils which can be justifiably insulated from market forces, and in relation to which the State has an important role. In outlining a number of challenges confronting this notion, I have indicated the considerable difficulties which such a line of argument must address. Perhaps the most significant of these challenges is the need for the underlying educational ideal implicit in the entitlement to be clarified and justified in the face of claims about the unavoidable heterogeneity of educational value.

In addressing such matters one is encountering issues central not only to markets in education, but to education itself.

References

BAILEY, C. (1992) 'Enterprise and liberal education: Some reservations', *Journal of Philosophy of Education*, 26, 1, pp. 99–106.

BALL, S. (1990) *Markets, Morality and Equality in Education*, Hillcole Group, Paper 5, London, The Tufnell Press.

BALL, S.J. (1993) 'Education markets, choice and social class: The market as a class strategy in the UK and the USA', *British Journal of Sociology of Education*, 14, 1, pp. 3–19

BOLTON, E. (1993) 'Perspectives on the National Curriculum', in O'HEAR, P. and WHITE, J. (Eds) *Assessing the National Curriculum*, London, Paul Chapman.

BRIDGES, D. (1992) 'Enterprise and liberal education', *Journal of Philosophy of Education*, 26, 1, pp. 91–8.

CARR, W. (1994) 'Education and Democracy: Confronting the Postmodernist Challenge', Paper presented to the Annual Conference of the Philosophy of Education Society of Great Britain, April.

CHUBB, J. and MOE, T. (1990) *Politics, Markets and America's Schools*, Washington DC, The Brookings Institution.

CHUBB, J. and MOE, T. (1992) *A Lesson in School Reform from Great Britain*, Washington DC, The Brookings Institution.

COHEN, B. (1981) *Education and the Individual*, London, Allen and Unwin.

COONS, J.E. and SUGARMAN, S.D. (1978) *Education by Choice: The Case For Family Control*, Berkeley, University of California Press.

COX, C., DOUGLAS-HUME, J., MARKS, J., NORCROSS, L. and SCRUTON, R. (1986) *Whose Schools? A Radical Manifesto*, London, The Hillgate Group.

DAVIES, J. (Ed) (1993) *God and the Marketplace. Essays on the Morality of Wealth Creation*, Choice in Welfare No 14, London, The Institute of Economic Affairs, Health and Welfare Unit.

FLEW, A. (1987) *Power to the Parents: Reversing Educational Decline*, London, The Sherwood Press.

GRACE, G. (1989) 'Education: Commodity or public good?', *British Journal of Educational Studies*, 37, 3, pp. 207–21.

GRAY, J. (1992) *The Moral Foundations of Market Institutions*, Choice in Welfare No 10, London, The Institute of Economic Affairs, Health and Welfare Unit.

GRAY, J. (1993) *Beyond the New Right. Markets, government and the common environment*, London, Routledge.

GREEN, A. (1991) 'The structure of the system: Proposals for change' in CHITTY, C. (Ed) *Changing the Future. Redprint for Education*, London, The Tufnell Press.

GREEN, D.G. (Ed) (1991) *Empowering the Parents: How to Break the Schools Monopoly*, Choice in Welfare No 9, London, The Institute of Economic Affairs, Health and Welfare Unit.

GUTMANN, A. (1987) *Democratic Education*, Princeton, Princeton University Press.

HALDANE, J. (Ed) (1992) *Education, Values and Culture. The Victor Cook Memorial Lectures*, St Andrews, Centre for Philosophy and Public Affairs, University of St Andrews.

HAYEK, F.A. (1960) *The Constitution of Liberty*, London, Routledge and Kegan Paul.

HEELAS, P. and MORRIS, P. (Eds) (1992) *The Values of the Enterprise Culture*, London, Routledge.

HIRST, P.H. (1993) 'Education, knowledge and practices', in BARROW, R. and WHITE, P. (Eds) *Beyond Liberal Education. Essays in honour of Paul H. Hirst*, London, Routledge.

HOLLIS, M. (1982) 'Education as a positional good', *Journal of Philosophy of Education*, 16, 2, pp. 235–44.

HOLLIS, M. (1989) 'Atomic energy and moral glue', *Journal of Philosophy of Education*, 23, 2, pp. 185–93.

HOLLIS, M. (1990) 'Market equality and social freedom', *Journal of Applied Philosophy*, 7, 1, pp. 15–23.

HOLLIS, M. (1992) 'Friends, romans and consumers', in MILLIGAN, D. and WATTS MILLER, W. (Eds) *Liberalism, Citizenship and Autonomy*, Aldershot, Avebury.

HOGAN, P. (1993) 'The practice of education and the courtship of youthful sensibility', *Journal of Philosophy of Education*, 27, 1, pp. 5–15.

INSTITUTE FOR PUBLIC POLICY RESEARCH (1993) *Education: A Different Vision. An Alternative White Paper*, London, Institute for Public Policy Research.

JONATHAN, R. (1986) 'Education and "The needs of society",' in HARTNETT, A. and NAISH, M. (Eds) *Education and Society Today*, London, The Falmer Press.

JONATHAN, R. (1989) 'Choice and control in education: Parental rights, individual liberties and social justice', *British Journal of Educational Studies*, 37, 4, pp. 321–38.

JONATHAN, R. (1990) 'State education service or prisoner's dilemma: The "Hidden Hand" as a source of education policy', *British Journal of Educational Studies*, 38, 2, pp. 116–32.

JONATHAN, R. (1993) 'Parental rights in schooling', in MUNN, P. (Ed) *Parents and Schools. Customers, Managers or Partners?*, London, Routledge.

KING, A.S. and REISS, M.J. (Eds) (1993) *The Multicultural Dimension of the National Curriculum*, London, The Falmer Press.

KUKATHAS, C. (1992) 'Freedom versus Autonomy', in GRAY, J. (1992), *The Moral Foundations of Market Institutions*, London, The Institute of Economic Affairs.

McLAUGHLIN, T.H. (1992a) 'Citizenship, diversity and education: A philosophical perspective', *Journal of Moral Education*, 21, 3, pp. 235–50.

McLAUGHLIN, T.H. (1992b) 'The ethics of separate schools', in LEICESTER, M. and TAYLOR, M.J. (Eds) *Ethics, Ethnicity and Education*, London, Kogan Page.

McLAUGHLIN, T.H. (1994) 'The scope of parents' educational rights', in HALSTEAD, J.M. (Ed) *Parental Choice and Education: Principles, Policy and Practice*, London, Kogan Page.

McMURTRY, J. (1991) 'Education and the market model', *Journal of Philosophy of Education*, 25, 2, pp. 209–17.

MILIBAND, D. (1991) *Markets, Politics and Education. Beyond the Education Reform Act*, Education and Training Paper No 3, London, Institute for Public Policy Research.

MILLIGAN, D. and WATTS MILLER, W. (Eds) (1992) *Liberalism, Citizenship and Autonomy*, Aldershot, Avebury.

NOVAK, M. (1991) *The Spirit of Democratic Capitalism*, London, The Institute of Economic Affairs, Health and Welfare Unit.

NOVAK, M. (1993) 'Eight arguments about the morality of the marketplace', in DAVIES, J. (Ed), *God and the Marketplace. Essays on the Morality of Wealth Creation*, London, The Institute of Economic Affairs.

O'HEAR, A. (1993) *An Entitlement to Knowledge. Agenda for the New Schools Authority*, Policy Study No 132, London, Centre for Policy Studies.

O'HEAR, P. and WHITE, J. (1991) *A National Curriculum for All: Laying the Foundations for Success*, Education and Training Paper No 6, London, Institute for Public Policy Research.

O'HEAR, P. and WHITE, J. (Eds) (1993) *Assessing the National Curriculum*, London, Paul Chapman.

PLANT, R. (1992a) 'Autonomy, social rights and distributive justice', in GRAY, J. (1992), op. cit.

PLANT, R. (1992b) Enterprise in its place: The moral limits of markets', in HEELAS, P. and MORRIS, P. (Eds) (1992) *The Values of the Enterprise Culture*, London, Routledge.

PLANT, R. and BARRY, N. (1990) *Citizenship and Rights in Thatcher's Britain: Two Views*, Choice in Welfare No 3, London, The Institute of Economic Affairs, Health and Welfare Unit.

RAWLS, J. (1993) *Political Liberalism*, New York, Columbia University Press.

SELDON, A. (1986) *The Riddle of the Voucher: An Inquiry into the Obstacles to Introducing Choice and Competition in State Schools*, London, The Institute of Economic Affairs.

TOOLEY, J. (1992a) 'The prisoner's dilemma and educational provision: A reply to Ruth Jonathan', *British Journal of Educational Studies*, 40, 2, pp. 118–33.

Terence H. McLaughlin

TOOLEY, J. (1992b) 'The "Pink Tank" on the education reform act', *British Journal of Educational Studies*, 40, 4, pp. 335–49.

TOOLEY, J. (1993a) *A Market-Led Alternative for the Curriculum: Breaking the Code*, The London File, London, Institute of Education University of London, Tufnell Press.

TOOLEY, J. (1993b) 'Education and "Public Goods": Markets versus the State', Paper presented to the Annual conference of the Philosophy of Education Society of Great Britain, April.

TOOLEY, J. (1993c) 'Equality of educational opportunity without the state?', *Studies in Philosophy and Education*, 12, 2–4, pp. 153–63.

WALZER, M. (1983) *Spheres of Justice: A Defence of Pluralism and Equality*, Oxford, Basil Blackwell.

WHITE, J. (1990) *Education and the Good Life: Beyond the National Curriculum*, London, Kogan Page.

WHITE, J. (1993) 'What place for values in the national curriculum?', in, O'HEAR, P. and WHITE, J. (Eds), *Assessing the National Curriculum*, London, Paul Chapman.

Notes on Contributors

David Bridges is Professor of Education at the University of East Anglia and has for the last five years directed the Eastern Region Teacher Education Consortium in the Employment Department Enterprise in Higher Education Initiative. It is particularly relevant to his chapter in this volume that he is also a parent and parent governor of an LEA maintained secondary school and he was for four years a co-opted member of Cambridgeshire Education Committee. His research interest in parent–school relations goes back to his work between 1979 and 1981 on the Cambridge Accountability Project (published in Elliott J. *et al. School Accountability*) and subsequent philosophical writing about parents' rights (for example 'Non paternalistic arguments in support of parents' rights' in *Journal of Philosophy of Education*, 18, 1, 1984).

Rosalie Clayton is Principal of Comberton Village College, Cambridgeshire. She is currently actively involved in a number of groups for grant maintained schools headteachers and has previously led training courses across the country for heads and deputies in Local Management of Schools. Prior to her school becoming grant maintained she was secretary of the Cambridgeshire LEA Association of Secondary Heads.

Peter Downes taught French at Manchester Grammar School and Banbury School and was prominent in the modern languages world as co-author of an audiovisual French course and as chairman for three years of the Annual Conference of the Joint Council of Language Associations. He was appointed Head of the Henry Box School, Witney, Oxfordshire in 1975. Since 1982, he has been Head of Hinchingbrooke School, Huntingdon, one of the pilot schools for local financial management in Cambridgeshire. He has taken a particular interest in the financing of education and contributes regularly to *Managing Schools Today* and to publications for heads and school governors by Croner Publications. On behalf of the Secondary Heads Association he contributed to the *LMS Initiative* publications by C.I.P.F.A. He was Salaries and Conditions of Service Officer for SHA and has been elected as president for the academic year 1994–5.

Philip Gardner is University Lecturer in Education and Fellow of St Edmund's College, Cambridge. He is a historian of education who is working on a book on the oral history of teaching in the early years of the twentieth century. His previous books include *The Lost Elementary Schools of Victorian England* and several school textbooks for the teaching of history.

Gerald Grace has taught at King's College, University of London, where he was director of the MA Urban Education programme, and at the University of Cambridge, where he was Fellow of Wolfson College. In 1987 he was appointed Professor and Head of the Department of Education at Victoria University of Wellington, New Zealand. In 1990 he was appointed professor and Head of the School of Education at Durham University. He is currently researching the changing nature of school leadership in England with particular reference to the position of headteachers.

Sheila Harty describes herself as a 'Nader Raider' having worked for ten years with Ralph Nader's Center for the Study of Responsive Law and, more recently, for the International Organisation of Consumers Unions based in Penang. She has a BA and MA in theology and is a freelance editor and writer in Washington DC. Her review of industry propaganda in schools entitled *Hucksters in the Classroom* won the George Orwell Award for Honesty and Clarity in Public Language.

Terence H. McLaughlin is University Lecturer in Education and Fellow of St Edmund's College, Cambridge. He specializes in philosophy of education and has written widely on such topics as parents' rights in upbringing and education, common and separate schools, pastoral care, values in education, and citizenship, diversity and education.

Geoff Morris was until recently Chief Education Officer in Cambridgeshire Local Education Authority. In this role he pioneered 'local financial management' and then 'local management of schools' and was responsible for the early establishment of LEA agencies. He now works as an educational consultant.

Donald Naismith has been the Director of Education of three London boroughs, and retired as Director of Education of the London borough of Wandsworth in March 1994, receiving a CBE for his services to education. He has been particularly concerned with the introduction of greater diversity of schools and parental and pupil choice.

Peter Roberts has been since 1978 when it opened, Head of Samuel Ward Upper School in Haverhill, Suffolk. From the start, he established a pattern of strong interchange and partnerships between the school and its community with a particular emphasis on school–industry links. He initiated the Sainsbury/ Suffolk Schools Industry Project.

James Tooley was a mathematics teacher for several years in Zimbabwe and England, before becoming a researcher for the National Foundation for

Educational Research. Subsequently he studied for his PhD in philosophy of education at the Institute of Education, University of London. He has been working in the Department of Educational Studies in the University of Oxford since January 1994.

John White is Professor of Philosophy of Education at the Institute of Education, University of London. His books include *Towards a Compulsory Curriculum, The Aims of Education Re-stated* and *Education and the Good Life: Beyond the National Curriculum.*

Colin Wringe is Senior Lecturer in Education at the University of Keele. He has written widely in philosophy of education and his books include *Children's Rights: A Philosophical Study, Democracy, Schooling and Political Education* and *Understanding Educational Aims.* He has also written extensively on the teaching of modern languages.

Index